Has anyone sung the song of the patient, calf-bearing, milk-flowing,
cud-chewing, tail-switching cow?
—Frank Lloyd Wright

The Complete Cow

Cow

Sara Rath

The cow is the foster mother of the human race. From the day of the ancient Hindoo to this time have the thoughts of men turned to this kindly and beneficent creature as one of the chief forces of human life.
—William Dempster Hoard, 1885

CRESTLINE

This edition published in 2011 by
CRESTLINE
a division of BOOK SALES, Inc.
276 Fifth Avenue Suite 206
New York, New York 10001
USA

This edition published by arrangement with Voyageur Press, Inc. 400 First Avenue North, Suite 300, Minneapolis, Minnesota, 55401

Edited by Michael Dregni
Designed by Kristy Tucker and Andrea Rud
Cover and cow migration map designed by Kristy Tucker
Printed in China

Library of Congress Cataloging-in-Publication Data
  Rath, Sara/
    The complete cow / Sara Rath.
      p. cm.
    Includes bibliographical references and index.
    1. Cattle. 2. Cattle breeds. 3. Cows I. Title.
  SF197.R22 1998
  636.2—dc21   98-11971
                                CIP

ISBN-13: 978-0-7858-2756-6

10 9 8 7 6 5 4 3 2 1

Printed in Hong Kong

Page 1, **Top left:** Edwin Megargee painting of a bovine beauty from 1928. **Top right:** "The cow jumped over the moon" from the children's rhyme "Hey, Diddle, Diddle." **Bottom right:** Who is it that said something about owners and their animals looking alike? (Minnesota State Fair collection)

Page 2: Guernsey beauty. (Photo © Lynn M. Stone)

Page 3: A farmer's best friend. (Minnesota State Fair collection)

Acknowledgments

As always, my appreciation to my husband, Del Lamont, and to my children, Jay Rath and Laura Rath Beausire, for their encouragement and support.

In researching this subject, I am indebted to animal scientists and professors in the United States, Canada, and Europe who shared their love of cattle and their vast knowledge, especially Paul Brackelsberg, Professor of Animal Science at Iowa State, Kevin Hill, Extension Livestock Agent for the University of Florida in Collier County, and Professor Larry Burditt and the folks who compile and maintain a wonderful Internet resource, the Oklahoma State Breeds of Livestock Page.

Photographers Bruce Fritz and Russell Graves came through whenever I asked for photos of specific breeds. And the Elm Grove Library rounded up every book I requested, no matter how obscure.

For help with the guide to mooing in different languages, thanks to Jeff Belcher at the University of Warwick.

Special thanks also to the vast number of breed associations, dairy farmers, and ranchers who went out of their way to provide pictures and information for this book.

Right: Ayrshire cow and calf engraving, 1877

Sara Rath

Contents

Above: Cow weather vane, 1883

Facing page: Angus cattle on the Bradley 3 Ranch, north of Childress, Texas. (Photo © Russell A. Graves)

For Whom Belle Toils

Ayrshire herd
Facing page: Cows may look as if they are just shuffling around haphazardly, but they are actually obeying a set of strict social rules. There is a rigid hierarchy in each herd: Every cow is a queen to all the cows below her, and the fawning subject of all the less dominant cows in the herd. (Photo © Lynn M. Stone)

Milking time
Right: A milkmaid puts her hands to the task.

Belle, a statuesque Ayrshire with mahogany spots, is being milked. I am seated on a low set of bleachers inside the Heritage Farm dairy complex at the Milwaukee County Zoo, in Milwaukee, Wisconsin, watching Belle, and the plastic tube through which her milk is pumped to a refrigerated, stainless-steel tank. Hermetically sealed off and separated by a clear sheet of glass, Belle seems oblivious to her audience, bored with the all-too-familiar routine. Every move of her life is analyzed in pixels and graphs: A computer chip suspended from her collar identifies her as she enters the milking parlor, and by the time Belle has finished milking, we will know how much more or less milk she gave now than she did last night.

Despite the presence of livestock nearby, there are no zoolike smells in this bright, octagonal barn—all the better for the Dairy Store to peddle pillowy cream puffs and towering ice cream cones. Behind the bleachers is a transparent plastic cow. From one of the white telephones next to it a solemn voice describes the process of digestion as the cow's colorful interior anatomy lights up, gullet to rumen, the first stomach, and back to the tongue, then the second, third, and fourth stomachs, and on to the bowel: the cow's digestive tract, lips to tail.

"We're a regular working dairy," the herdsman assures his audience over a microphone. "We're milking five cows right now, and sell our milk to Golden Guernsey. We average 500 pounds [225 kg] of milk, every other day."

In addition to Belle, the zoo's dairy herd consists of a Milking Shorthorn, Brown Swiss, and both red-and-white and black-and-white Holsteins. I saw a Jersey at a feed bunker by the front door, along with an Ayrshire heifer (Belle's calf) and a black-and-white Holstein calf. This is the closest herd of cows to my home in Elm Grove, Wisconsin, no more than three miles (5 km) away over dense urban territory if I were a crow. And I am amused by the presence of cows in a zoo right here in Wisconsin, the heartland of "America's Dairyland," as if they were an endan-

gered species.

Ironically, a hundred years ago, a woman named Adda Howie was raising one of the country's largest and finest herds of purebred Jerseys in Elm Grove, but any remnants of Mrs. Howie and her prizewinning Jerseys are long gone. When I asked at the Village Hall where Howie's Sunny Peak Farm was, no one knew what I was talking about. Yet the honors received by Sunny Peak Farm became so widely known at the turn of the century that the Japanese government purchased a carload of Adda Howie's Jerseys to improve its livestock—the first Jerseys imported into Japan. Howie twice traveled to the Isle of Jersey to study their methods of dairying, and in 1914, it was written that "Mrs. Howie is one of the most famous women in the United States—one about whom more has been written and printed in this and foreign countries than about any other woman now living . . . and she believes that cattle are the noblest of all God's creation in the animal kingdom."

At the zoo, I order some ice cream—butter pecan—and wonder how many more years will pass before zoo exhibits like Heritage Farm will be only romanticized relics of a once-common way of life. Already, farmers in the western United States and other parts of the world think nothing of milking thousands of cows per day. Their milking machines never stop running. There are no grassy meadows on these factory-farms, no idyllic scenes of cows grazing beside the requisite babbling brook: just cows loafing in huge pens munching high-grade feed and producing incredible amounts of milk.

I grew up in farming country in central Wisconsin, but I was not raised on a

Milking time

As his son lovingly pets the family's cow, an Old Order Amish farmer milks, and the cat waits for his share. (Photo © Jerry Irwin)

farm. Only three or four miles away (5–6 km), our cousins had Lindsay's Farm, and I often begged Grandpa Lindsay to take me there. It was at Lindsay's Farm, at the age of five, that I was offered my first drink of milk straight from a cow. Inside the great red dairy barn, the unfamiliar aromas of silage and manure mingled with the creamy scent of frothy milk in the upturned cap of a milk can my cousin handed to me. The cow's udder looked rubbery. The milk was warm, as warm as the cow. I began to perspire.

Enormous black and white rumps lined either side of the narrow aisle, tails switching, flies buzzing, hooves stomping, cow pies splattering. Prince, that fearsome bull near the door (I couldn't escape without passing his pen again!) butted the metal bars with his gigantic Holstein head. Somewhere in the haymow was a damp nest of new kittens that I desperately wanted to find. I hated warm milk, but sipped it with a shudder. Everyone smiled when the milk dribbled past my lips, onto my overalls. When I finally found the kittens, they wouldn't stop licking me.

Back in the Heritage Farm barnyard now, a furry Belted Galloway lies in dappled sunlight, casually chewing her cud. A red Highland heifer scratches an itch on her hip with the tip of her elegant horns, her friendly face almost hidden by shaggy ringlets falling over her eyes.

Butter pecan is still my favorite flavor, I decide, marveling at my capacity to enjoy ice cream while the redolence of cows and other zoo aromas invades my nostrils. I stand with elbows on the barnyard fence, embracing the sunshine and the languid cattle, searching for a phrase that will capture the profound signifi-

cance of dairy cows and exotic breeds maintained by a zoo. There is an important paradox here, I am convinced, but words elude me this lazy afternoon, so I simply enjoy the day and the ice cream and remember a joke I recently heard.

The joke, from an Australian radio program, "The Club Cow," broadcasting from Melbourne on Saturday nights, goes like this:

A man drives into a gas station and has his tank filled up. While running the pump, the clerk spots two cows sitting in the back seat of the car. He asks the driver what he's up to with the two cows in his back seat. The driver has asked himself the same question.

Clerk: "You should take them to the zoo."

The man thinks this is a good idea and drives away.

The next day he arrives at that same gas station with the cows still in the back seat. Clerk: "I thought you would take them to the zoo!"

Driver: "Yes, we had a swell day yesterday. Today I'm taking them to the beach."

Adda Howie with Jersey calf
Wisconsin's famous Adda Howie at work on Sunny Peak Farm in Elm Grove. As was written about her in 1914, "She believes that cattle are the noblest of all God's creation in the animal kingdom." (State Historical Society of Wisconsin)

The Spirit of Moo

The cow is of the bovine ilk;
One end is moo, the other milk.
—Ogden Nash, "The Cow," 1930

Content Holstein
Facing page: A Holstein chews its cud and surveys its dominion. (Photo © Lynn M. Stone)

Isis with cow's horns
Right: The Egyptian goddess of fertility and motherhood circa 1323 B.C., Isis was always represented as a woman with cow's horns. She was the mother of Horus, the god of sky, light, and goodness. The cult of Isis spread from Alexandria to all the Mediterranean countries, especially Greece and Rome, reaching a peak in the third century B.C.

"I have a real good *moo*," someone told me the other day, "you know, when you see a herd of cows next to the road and you pull the car over and open the window and call *mOOOooo*."

Many people actually do this. And cows, friendly and inquisitive creatures that they are, will lift their heads, green grass stuck to wet lips, and send a congenial *moo* right back.

It must be a common curiosity, this desire to communicate with cows. "Here a *moo*, there a *moo*, everywhere a *moo, moo*"—even on the

Internet. If you're adept at downloading, you can choose the *moo* of your choice from several bovine-related Web pages and moo back to your heart's delight. From among a variety of selections, you may choose a "Chorus of *Moos*," "A very distinct *moo*," a "Very nice *moo*," an "Emphatic *moo*," or "A long, soulful *moo*."

Cave paintings
The aurochs in this reproduction of the famed Lascaux cave paintings may be found in the *Salle des Taureaux*, or Room of the Bulls, located in Lascaux II in the Dordogne region of France. The Lascaux cave aurochs, created 17,000 years ago, were discovered by accident in 1940 when a dog belonging to neighborhood boys fell into a hole leading to the underground chamber. Art historians feel certain that these paintings, hidden in a secret location far from the entrance to the grotto, were produced as part of a magic ritual to ensure a successful hunt.

A *cowskin*, besides being the skin of a cow, is also another name for an ancient kind of prophylactic. In 1738, men were admonished that "A good Cowskin, Crabtree or Bulls pizzle may be plentifully bestow'd on your outward Man."

On the other hand, if you prefer to *moo* in solitude without artificial stimulation, you can adapt a variety of cow tongues and translate *moo* in different languages with the help of this handy guide:

How to Say *Moo* in Eleven Languages

Danish: *Muuh*
Finnish: *Ammuu*
French: *Meuh*
German: *Muh*
Hebrew: *Go'eh*
Italian: *Mu!*
Japanese: *Mo* (as in "mow" the grass)
Norwegian: *Mø*
Portuguese (Brazilian): *Muuu*
Swedish: *Muu*
Welsh: *Moo*

That we are drawn to *moo* is not a recent phenomenon. The sound may subliminally remind us of the dawn of civilization: a tranquil, pastoral ideal where peace and contentment were found in green pastures beside still waters, far from worldly strife and turmoil. The reassurance of *moo* meant all was well with the world.

Even simpler than that, perhaps we are just pleased to realize that cows are interactive. They respond with agreeable ease. Or maybe *moo* is comforting because it recalls our childhood, learning the answer to "What does the cow say?" and being praised for our brilliance when we knew what to reply.

To Speak is Human; To *Moo*, Bovine

Creation myths from a variety of cultures speak of a time when humans and animals spoke the same language. Perhaps influenced by that thought, succeeding eons have encouraged us to attune to animals by mimicking their sounds.

It's a known fact that animals communicate among themselves, with other animals, and with us. Sometimes this language is interpreted scientifically, and sometimes symbolically—as in bovine adages, such as "When a cow tries to scratch her ear, It means a shower is very near. . . ."

If you are a cow watcher, it won't take long before you discover that the *moo* for "Get out of my way" is different than the *moo* for "Isn't it time for breakfast?" or "Hey, you stepped on my udder!" In fact, cows communicate sounds to express a variety of moods, such as hunger (especially calves), distress calls (the bellowing of a bull), sexual behavior and related fighting, and mother-calf interrelations to establish contact and evoke maternal behavior. Cattle also *moo* to help maintain the herd in its movements. Scientists have identified at least six different cattle vocalizations, depending on the level of excitation in the animal.

Our almost inborn desire to *moo* at cows may embody more than just a curious need to cause a cow to *moo* in return. An enormous realm of ritual traditions passed down through the fog of generations and societies embrace animal rites and ceremonies that involve unique symbols and energies. More than one of these rituals involves learning the language of the animal to which you are drawn.

Zuni Indians were early practitioners of this art: They had ceremonies to summon their Beast Gods, and wore ritual masks, danced, shook rattles, and drummed. Anthropologists observing the rites claimed the Pueblo Indian dancers were doing much more than simply impersonating animal forms; they were transported into an altered state of consciousness by their actions, becoming for the time being the actual embodiment of the spirit which was believed to reside in the mask.

If you feel compelled to adopt an animal totem, you are invited to imitate the animal's movements, postures, and gestures. Cows lie around in the grass, chew their cud, look at the world with indifference, adapt a placid attitude. Couldn't we all use a little more of that?

For a better description of "The Similitude of the Cow," Jared Van Wagenen, Jr., wrote this vivid word-portrait in *The Cow* in 1922: "Once before you, the cow is a ponderous bulky beast, the very mass of her—if she is of the big breeds—striking fear into the minds of the timid as they see her rise. She seems to shake the ground. The huge bulk conveys an impression of angularity,—a massive rectangle with projecting prominences at the hips and above the front legs. . . . The most graceful part of the animal is the upper neck, attractive in conformation, flexible, soft and pleasant to the feel; it is about the neck that one wants to throw the arm, for a cow responds to affection."

As you mimic her movements, however, keep in mind that cows look funny when they run. And cows cannot belch, so they have a tremendous problem with flatulence. Cows drool. They have no front teeth on the top jaw, only on the bottom. And when they lie down, they free-fall fifteen to eighteen inches (375–450 mm).

But even Van Wagenen claims that "Intellectually and morally, a very good case cannot be made out for the cow. Her standards of ethics and honor are low. In her conduct toward the other members of the herd she is both cruel and cowardly. Cattle by nature are polygamous, roving in herds with an old bull at the head who holds his place against all comers by ordeal of combat." However, he says, "Cow life is not quite all eating and fighting. Cows greatly enjoy licking all parts of the body that they can reach, this probably being the bovine ideal of a careful toilet. It is rather amusing to see another cow very carefully bestowing this attention on the head and face of a neighbor who, of course, cannot reach them with her own tongue. It is hard to decide whether the giver or the recipient derives most pleasure from this service."

In addition to getting one's face licked by a bovine neighbor, being milked twice a day by a machine doesn't sound like any picnic, either. And then there's the matter of that cud they chew and chew and chew most of the day; it has been regurgitated back up from their first stomach and is eventually swallowed again. Still, it would be rather cool to be able to slide one's tongue up one's nose, a nostril at a time. And some cattle, like horses, have a well-developed subcutaneous muscle layer that allows them to shake localized areas of their skin to dislodge insects without switching their tail.

On the Importance of Cows

Early scholars didn't know much about the origin of things, and even if they understood about the birds, they were

Roman coin
The Latin word for money, *pecunia*, from which the words *pecuniary* and *impecunius* are derived, and the word *fee* both come from the old word *pecus*, meaning "cattle." Here, the image of a bull is stamped onto a Roman coin.

mighty confused about the bees. Greek poet Philetas (330 B.C.–270 B.C.) believed that bees were born from the putrefied flesh of oxen, and called them "oxborn bees." Other "spontaneous generation" doctrines claimed that frogs were born from slime, crickets sprouted from chimneys, wasps sprung from dead horses, and worms grew from dirt. According to English poet John Milton in *Paradise Lost* (1667), however, the cow was created by divine hand on the sixth day:

> The Sixt, and of Creation last arose
> With Evening Harps and Mattin, when God said,
> Let th' Earth bring forth Soul living in her kind,
> Cattel and Creeping things, and Beast of th' Earth,
> Each in their kind. The Earth obey'd and strait
> Op'ning her fertil Woomb teem'd at a Birth
> innumerous living Creatures, perfet formes,
> Limb'd and full grown: out of the ground up rose
> As from his Lair the wild Beast where he wonns
> In Forest wild, in Thicket, Brake, or Den;
> among the Trees in Pairs they rose, they walk'd:
> The Cattel in the Fields and Meddows green:
> Those rare and solitarie, these in flocks
> Pasturing at once, and in broad Herds upsprung.
> The grassie Clods now Calv'd....

Angus moo

Above: An Angus cow stretches its neck and lows. (Photo © Russell A. Graves)

Anatomy of a *moo*

Left: Scientists have identified at least six different cattle vocalizations, depending on the level of excitation in the animal. Cows communicate to express hunger and distress; the bellowing of a bull may express sexual behavior and related fighting; and mothers and calves may communicate to establish contact and evoke maternal behavior. Cattle also moo to help maintain the herd in its movements. These graphs, derived from *Communication and Expression in Hoofed Mammals* by Fritz R. Walther, depict the syllables of cattle lows and the way they combine to form the calls.

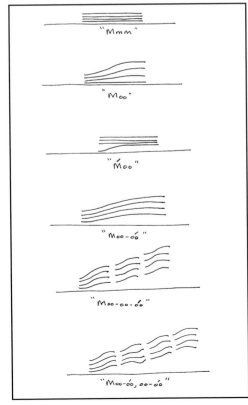

No matter how they were created, cows were at first wild animals that we now know as aurochs. They were hunted, just as all wild animals were hunted; at a later date, they became domesticated. No one is actually clear about how that happened, but it may have been during the transitional period of prehistory when humans underwent a shift from hunter to pastoralist and the hunters brought home the offspring of the species they slew. The hunters may have thought a calf was too small and useless for meat and hide, or they may have felt sympathy for the motherless creature and brought it back to the cave for their own families to play with and to raise. The outcome was evident: In the early days of our existence, we became a cattle culture. The proof is in the language we still use everyday, words derived from terms once related to cattle.

The word *daughter* corresponds to the Greek *thaughter* and Sanskrit *duhitar*, meaning "milker," because women who milked the cows were highly valued.

In Sanskrit, *soldier* meant "one who fights about cows." *Morning* was "the

"Wealth in small cattle"

In ancient Ireland, wealth was referred to neither in terms of money nor ownership of land; instead, the cow was the measure of everything, including the unit of value. An old saying was, "He who is born on Monday, his wealth in cattle will be good. He who is born on Tuesday . . . great will be his wealth in small cattle." (Photo © David Lorenz Winston)

The Mythical Cow

From the beginning of time, myths concerning cows and bulls have been prevalent around the world. The cow generally embodied lunar aspects; the bull symbolized the sun.

India: In the long history of India, it is only relatively recently that devout Hindus have accorded the cow special sanctity. Throughout the Vedic period, for instance, cattle had an important ritualistic role in Vedic sacrifice, where they were the principal sacrificial victims and their flesh was consumed afterward by priests. Cattle were also commonly used in metaphorical allusions, and the cow was referred to as a mother goddess; the bull a natural symbol of virility.

In India today, Hindus believe the cow is sacred, and cattle are treated with great respect. Cows are described as the mothers of all beings, or as children of the sun. The cow world is considered to be the highest and greatest of all worlds. A house is pitied if it has not a single cow; the exhaled breath of cows causes peace within a house. The sale of cows is prdhibited, and anyone who would sell a cow is considered as evil as someone who would sell their own mother. A person who kills a cow becomes a ghost and has to experience twenty-one kinds of hell.

One sacred story involves the culture hero, Prithu, who wanted to find edible plants for his subjects. When he attacked the earth, it assumed the shape of a cow and fled through the heavens. Finally, the cow yielded and promised to "fecundate the earth with milk." Svāyambhuva Manu, the calf, was created, and the earth was milked. The *Rig-Veda* alludes to the mystical relationship between the cow and the earth, and in India the five products of the cow—milk, curds, clarified butter, urine, and cow dung—are also considered pure and are used in purfication ceremonies. During festivals, cows are painted with ritual designs and decorated with beautiful garlands. Lakshmi, goddess of fortune, is associated with milk, so such a drink should not be refused. Brahma is depicted riding upon a cow; Indra, another Hindu divine being, is depicted as riding upon a bull. The bull Nandi was ridden by the Hindu god, Shiva. The cow is the symbol of the multi-armed goddess Kali, and goddesses Aditi and Prithivi are also related to cows in their aspects of fertility.

Egypt: The Egyptians possessed a cult of cow worship perhaps even more ancient than the cow adoration of India: Apis, the most sacred bull of Egypt, was brought by boat to Memphis in a cabin lined with gold. There he was kept in a temple near the temple of Ptah. Apis (also referred to Hap) was believed to be the reincarnation of Ptah, a god who had assumed the disguise of a celestial fire, inseminated a virgin heifer, and fathered a black bull calf with mystical markings who was actually Ptah returned to earth. Apis was fed and watered at a certain hour each day, while his devoted followers watched and worshiped. When this bull died, another calf had to be found with special markings that identified it as the

Minotaur
The Minotaur had a crowned man's head and the body of a bull with wings. This image came from an Assyrian and Sumero-Semitic sculpture. The Assyrians called this being the Shedim or Shedu, and carved his image in stone as the guardian of the gates and doors of their temples and palaces.

successor. For forty days thereafter, the new calf was attended by women who stood before him, lifted their robes and displayed themselves in a sexual manner.

Apis may have belonged to Ptah, but he was also connected with Osiris, whose body some Egyptian paintings depict as being carried by a black bull and who is often rendered with the head of a bull. Later Egyptian rulers, the Ptolemies, combined Apis and Osiris to create Sarapis, another deity.

Buchis, also a sacred bull of the Egyptians, had a hide that changed color every hour. Hathor, the Great Mother, created the Milky Way with milk from her udder. She was served by Egyptian princesses who were assimilated to cowlike forms.

When an Egyptian princess died, her body was buried in a cow-shaped sarcophagus or buried with a sacred bull, a custom that may be interpreted as a kind of symbolic marriage; a mummified bull's phallus found in the tomb of a princess encourages this hypothesis. The Egyptian *Book of the Dead* describes the ancient practice of wrapping the dead in a bull's hide for magical purification.

The Egyptian goddess Nut, the Celestial Cow, wore stars on her belly. Isis, sometimes wore a cow-head or horns similar to the Phoenician moon-goddess, Astarte. There was a tendency, in classical antiquity, to equate the gods of one religion with those of another, so identities are sometimes confusing.

Crete: The ancient Cretans held the bull in high esteem. It was believed that a bull's virility was concentrated in its horns. Bull sacrifices and bull acrobatics were recorded on the murals of the palace of Knossos. Bull dances (called the *Taurokathapsia*), vividly depicted in the temples, were performed to honor the bull and what they felt the bull represented. Bull-leapers in these ceremonies may have been predecessors of today's bullfighters. Kings wore bull masks and were considered spiritually related to the bull during this festival. At the conclusion of the ritual, the Cretan Moon Bull was sacrificed in place of the king. The sacred *labyrs*, or "lip," was an extremely holy Cretan goddess symbol and was utilized in the bull sacrifice.

Greece: Because the Minoan culture on Crete preceded that of Greece, many of the bull legends of Crete became interwoven in Greek mythology. Zeus, the supreme god of Greek myth (who became known as Jupiter to the Romans) possessed irresistible power and uninhibited sexuality. He could also manifest himself in various disguises, and frequently, when he was intent on rape, changed himself into a bull. When Zeus desired Demeter and she refused him, Zeus changed himself into a bull and raped her—from which act the goddess Persephone was born. Zeus became a bull again when he raped Europa, who then gave birth to Minos, who became King of Crete.

Minos, perhaps due to his unusual conception, was somewhat haunted by bulls. His queen, Pasiphae, after having borne him several normal children, became impassioned with sexual desire for a certain bull. Pasiphae asked Dedalus, the master-craftsman of that era, to construct a dummy cow. Pasiphae hid herself in the cow, lying in wait to seduce the bull. The result of this union was the Minotaur, half-human, half-bull. Her husband, Minos, was not pleased, and he condemned the Minotaur to an underground labyrinth at Knossos, where he could survive only upon a diet of human flesh. This was provided by the annual contribution of seven Athenian youths and seven Athenian maidens, but the sacrifice came to an end, when the hero, Theseus, met and slew the Minotaur.

Rome: Words of brides at ancient Roman weddings included, "Where thou art the Bull, I am the Cow." This has also been reported in ceremonies from the heroic literature of the Celts, and in fertility rites among the Kurds where the priest announced to the congregation that he was the Great Bull, and the woman recently married replied that she was the Young Cow. At this point, the lights were doused and the congregation indulged in a massive orgy.

Italy means "calf-land," and is therefore tied to Hera, the Great Mother, in her form as a cow. The cornucopia, the "horn of plenty," was used by Romans to symbolize good things given by the Great Cow.

Turkey was the birthplace of the religion of Mithraism, which spread to western Europe and finally to Rome, where it grew to be quite powerful and threatened the birth of Christianity.

Mithra appeared on earth from the face of a rock. He was born on December 25, and shepherds watching their flocks heralded his birth. There are many strange resemblances to Christ, although, according to Plutarch, Mithriasm appeared in Rome as early as 67 B.C. and rose to its peak over three centuries later, in 308 A.D. Mithra was considered to be a god of light, justice, and truth, and after his death, he ascended into heaven from whence he was to return on the final day of judgment to judge the quick and the dead.

While on earth, Mithra performed many miracles, but his adventures with a white bull brought him the greatest admiration and became the sacred symbol of his creed: One day Mithra was walking through a pasture and saw a magnificent white bull grazing. He decided to capture the bull alive with his own bare hands. He seized the bull by the horns and mounted him. He rode the bull and fought him until the bull collapsed, and then he dragged the bull to his cave. This painful journey of Mithra over rugged terrain became symbolic of human suffering on earth. Bull sacrifices were held by followers of Mithras, and initiates were bathed in the blood of a sacrificed bull to symbolize death and resurrection.

Mithraian shrines have been found wherever the Roman legions marched, from the banks of the Black Sea to the mountains of Scotland and the borders of the Sahara Desert. Germany has the most numerous and richest of Mithraic relics.

England: The Druids, who performed human sacrifices, used bulls for religious purposes when humans were not available. Pliny described it thus:

"Having made preparation for sacrifice and a banquet beneath the trees, they bring thither two white bulls, whose horns are bound then for the first time. Clad in a white robe the priest ascends the tree and cuts the mistletoe with a golden sickle, and it is received by others in a white cloak. They then kill the victims, praying that God will render this gift of his propitious to those to whom he has granted it."

The Druids considered white bulls especially holy, and today's White Park Cattle are thought to be the special white cattle they preferred. Within the alphabet of twenty letters used by the Druids in the sixth century B.C., the first letter is the letter Beth, for B, which represents the birch tree. Its color is white; its deity is the White Goddess, Belin; its bird is the pheasant; its herb is the Fly Agaric mushroom; its animal is the white cow, and birch is used for cradles, broomsticks, and yule logs.

Scandinavia: The Scandinavians had their own cow-legend surrounding the myth of Audhumla, the Great Cow, who licked the giants and gods into existence from great blocks of ice. Nerthus, the Earth Mother, made her yearly journey across the land in a cart that was drawn by sacred cows.

calling of the cattle," and *evening* was "the milking-time."

Stock (as in "stocks and bonds") refers to the use of cattle or "live stock," as currency. In old Anglo-Saxon, movable property was called *cwichfeoh*, or "living cattle," whereas immovable property, such as buildings and land, translated as "dead cattle." *Chattel*, meaning "nonliving personal property," came from the word *catel*, which was used in the sense of "wealth." And the words for *prince, king, lord,* and so forth, all meant "herdsman" or "head of pastoral family."

As recently as 1901, an enormous stone monument was exhumed on the site of Sushan, as mentioned in the Hebrew book of Esther. This monument contained the written laws of Hamurabi, the most illustrious king of the first dynasty of Babylon, who reigned from 2285 B.C. to 2242 B.C., and in the Book of Genesis is referred to as King Amraphel. The Code of Hamurabi reveals a Babylonian civilization in the third millennium B.C. governed by laws that were apparently received from the sun god Samas, "the judge of heaven and earth." About

Black Baldies on their way home
"Till the cows come home" is a jocular phrase used in a multitude of plays, poems, and stories. The line perhaps began with an English play from 1610, *The Scornful Lady*, which included the line, "Kiss till the cow comes home." (Photo © Russell A. Graves)

Bovine Taxonomy

A rose is a rose is a rose, but a cow is not necessarily always simply a cow. To begin with, a *cow* is the mature female of a bovine animal, genus *Bos*. The whole cow "family" is usually known as "cattle." A *heifer* is kind of like a cow, but it's not a *true* cow, yet, and won't actually be a cow, won't begin to have her birthdays recorded or even be taken seriously as a cow, until she has given birth to her first calf. And don't go around pointing at a bull and calling it a cow, or you can get into real trouble. Bulls are rather macho creatures, and they aren't cows any more than men are women. A *bull* is, strictly speaking, an adult male bovine animal. A *steer* is a young ox, especially one castrated before maturity and raised for beef. An *ox* is an adult castrated bull.

Egyptian clay tablets dating over 4,000 years ago refer to cheese used as a tax imposed on conquered tribes.

Statuesque cows
Simmental/Hereford crossbred cows graze and gaze. (Photo © David Lorenz Winston)

Affectionate Ayrshires

An Ayrshire cow scratches another's neck. (Photo © Lynn M. Stone)

one-seventh of the legible sections in the code refer to cattle, sheep, or livestock. Herdsmen were to be well-compensated for their work, hired by the year, and paid in units of grains with which to make bread. The duties and responsibilities of the cowboy and shepherd of Hamurabi's day were sharply defined in these laws. For example: If a man has hired an ox and through neglect or blows has caused it to die, ox for ox to the owner of the ox shall he render. If a man has hired an ox and has crushed its horn, cut off its tail,

or pierced its nostrils, he shall pay a quarter of its price.

Virtually from the beginning, livestock became humanity's chief interest, our main source of wealth and the principal means of exchange. Everything, from a new coat to a new idol or a new wife, was priced at so many cows. Cows led us from a state of savagery to a higher plane of existence, pulling our plows, drawing our carts, giving us milk and meat. The influence of cattle upon the mental development and material ad-

Bovine ecstasy
A Holstein cow scratches itself against a tree.
(Photo © David Lorenz Winston)

Legend tells of an Arabian merchant who, before starting on a journey, placed milk inside a water-pouch made of a sheep's stomach. During the day, the combination of the sun's heat and the rennet in the lining of the stomach changed the milk into cheese curd and whey.

vancement of humanity is immeasurable, and lingers, still.

Marriage dowries running far back in time and in many parts of the world arranged for the payment of large numbers of cows. Cows were used for paying fines, especially in terms of damages to the family of someone who had been slain. Cows were asked as ransom for release of a prestigious prisoner. One of the largest ransoms on record said to have been paid in 1029 for Olaf, son of Sitric, King of the Norse in Ireland, included 1,200 cows.

The most impoverished person was the person with only one cow; the wealth of the richest consisted of vast herds. When referring to an ancient Irish king or a chieftain who, having been engaged in war, concluded a treaty with his enemy, it was said, "And he made peace for the sake of his cows and his people."

Early poets depended upon their patrons for support, and in Ireland poems were held in high regard. "The poet gives poems of praise to the patron, who in turn bestows largesse upon the poet,"

Sitting cow

A Holstein cow prepares for a leisurely afternoon. (Photo © Lynn M. Stone)

The Greek writer, Otesia, referred in 400 B.C. to the legend of the Assyrian queen Semiramis, whom birds fed with cheese stolen from shepherds.

---

raised for breeding purposes or to provide oxen for plowing.

A practice felt to have been spread by the first cattle-keeping people in Neolithic times and found in Ireland, Scotland, India, and Africa, and in regions inhabited by the Mongols (but unknown in Germany or England) involved the belief that the calf had to be present during milking or a cow wouldn't let down her milk. If something happened to the calf—if it had been slaughtered to save milk or had been eaten—the calfskin was stuffed and placed beside the cow, and she accepted it as her actual calf. If nothing else worked, the milkmaid—for only women were allowed to milk the cows—was encouraged to sing. "The last remedy used to pacify her (the cow) is to use the sweetest voice and sing all the time of milking her," according to Lucas.

Another unusual custom found in ancient Ireland, Russia, Egypt, China, India, and Africa, was cow-blowing. A seventeenth-century Irish writer described it like this: "The women wash their hands in Cowes dung, and so gently stroke their dugges [teats], yea, put their hands into the cowes taile, and with their mouthes blow into their tailes, that with this maner [as it were] of inchantment, they may draw milk to them." Granted, this is a rather vague picture. The fact is, the women blew into the cow's vagina, "as much wind as they can, with which doing they many times come off with a shitten nose." The object of this bizarre behavior was to apparently inflate the cow's veins with air and so cause the udder to be forced down.

A similar practice witnessed in the efforts of the Waniaturu tribe of Africa in 1916 was described in this way: "If a

writes A. T. Lucas in *Cattle in Ancient Ireland*. Poets existed on a reciprocal gift-giving basis, with the gifts to the poets frequently consisting of cattle. In 1298, a poet wrote of a patron's daughter, "For these words addressed to her thick locks I demand her good kine [cow] in return." The poets were graded according to skill, with the highest grade, or ollamh poet, entitled to a maximum of ten cows and a heifer.

Because of the importance of cattle in Irish culture, unusual customs were recorded that were evidenced in other countries, as well. During the pre-Christian era, it was said that when a child was born, the father or another person immediately immersed it in water three times, but if it was the child of a rich man it was immersed three times in milk. In Ireland, cows were used mostly for milk. In fact, most, if not all, bull calves were killed at birth—except for those intended to be

In Roman times, cheese was made in Italy, but the most important source was the Alpine region of Switzerland. Roman patricians obtained a variety of cheese from different areas of their empire.

Texas Longhorn
Charles M. Russell, considered by many as the greatest painter of the American Wild West, loved to paint Texas Longhorns. "When it comes to making the beautiful Ma Nature has man beat all ways from the ace," he wrote in a letter collected in *Good Medicine*. "I have made a living painting the horned animal that the old lady I'm talking about made . . . I would starve to death painting the hornless deformity that man has made." (Photo © Lynn M. Stone)

cow refuses to be milked, a witch doctor (the *mbahangombe*) brews a secret concoction with which he smears the hind quarters of the animal around the vulva. Thereupon he takes some of the brew in his mouth and holding the lips of the vulva wide apart blows it vigorously into the vagina. The cow reacting to these interventions, arches her back and urinates in his face, a circumstance which appears to be of little consequence to the operator. At the same time, the witch doctor drapes a calf's skin over a small boy who has been smeared previously with the concoction and places him before the cow; the animal smells the pelt, licks it, and soon submits quietly to the milking routine. Indeed, so accustomed may the cow become to the presence of the child that she will become restless and bellow loudly if the substitute is not to hand."

In 1945, a man in County Kerry, Ireland, remembered that after calving some cows became ill, with consequent reduction in their yield of milk. Women and old people maintained that these symptoms were due to the fact that they had not yet passed the runncallach, a fluid resembling thick blood. To induce the cow to pass the blood, a woman blew three puffs of her breath into the cow's vagina. The man said, "I often saw my mother dow it with cows that did not pass the runncallach; after three or four days [following calving] she would blow into them and they would pass it the next day."

A Case for Bulls

If cows were treated with unusual care and affection, bulls were often given a much more difficult time. Frequently, bull calves were killed at birth so the cow would have more milk for the family. Occasionally, a meal of "staggering bob" was prepared by Irish families—this was veal from a two- or three-day-old calf. The name was thought to be derived from the fact that the animal wasn't old enough to stand on its own two legs. The dish consisted of meat scalded with water and then fried with bacon. The poorer the owner of the cow, the greater the need to dispose of the calf, particularly if it was male.

Some bulls were raised for breeding purposes, and some reached adulthood to be castrated and used as oxen. To be "as strong as an ox" has always implied inordinate strength. The truth is, a full-grown ox, in good condition, is truly a powerful animal. In most parts of the world, the first and most essential role for cattle was to provide muscle power—to help with cultivation, to draw carts or heavy timber, or to carry packs or people on their backs. The ability and willingness for oxen to work remains the most important quality of cattle in many regions even today, especially in third-world countries where farming is at a subsistence level. Such animals are only eaten

Bareback steer riding
Riding a bucking steer at roundup time was one of the few diversions in the life of a cowboy, and later give birth to the modern rodeo. This illustration was drawn from a photograph by C. D. Kirkland of Cheyenne, Wyoming, and appeared in the famous *Frank Leslie's Illustrated Newspaper* in 1888.

(if at all) when they are no longer fit for work, and they are often milked only incidentally, after the calves have had their fill, to provide a sustenance for the home. In most cultures, milk was normally taken from sheep and goats, rather than from cattle.

Another important remnant of the oxen's influence is experienced by many of us everyday: a furlong is the length of a furrow an ox was expected to plow between rests. Thus, the medieval English ox gave us the measure of the familiar,

but arbitrary, English mile we live by: namely, eight furlongs in length.

As tough as oxen had it, other bulls would have been happy to trade lots. In the 1200s in England, some bulls were set aside for the sport of bull-running. During the reign of King John, the town of Stamford, Lincolnshire, turned a bull loose in the marketplace every November 13 at 11 A.M. The idea of the sport was for men and boys to pursue the bull with clubs, trying to drive it up on the bridge, where the most courageous of the crowd

Forecasting the weather

Old wives' tales claim cows can forecast the weather: "When a cow tries to scratch her ear, it means a shower is very near. When she thumps her ribs with her tail, look out for thunder, lightning and hail." But when a cow sticks her tongue up her nose, who knows? (Photo © Bruce Fritz)

seized the animal and grasped its horns, trying to make it fall into the river. Eventually the bull would swim to shore and there it would be slaughtered; its meat was sold to the men and boys who had been in the run. The sport of bull-running lasted in Stamford for almost 650 years, until it was abolished in 1840.

Bull-baiting was another entertainment in old England, a sport in which bulls were teased by bulldogs that bit the pad of the bull's nose and hung on as the bull tried to shake the dog off. In the 1570s, Queen Elizabeth was said to have attended a bull or bear baiting every Sunday afternoon. Many claimed that the Queen's subjects preferred entertainments at the bear "gardens" to the plays of Shakespeare being performed next door, and continental travelers commented that the English seemed peculiarly addicted to such amusements. (References to bulls and bears in this entertainment may have been the origin of our references to the stock market being "bullish" or "bearish," depending on the activity or lack of same.)

Bullfights, on the other hand, developed through history from early mythology and bull cults in India, Persia, Mesopotamia, Egypt, Greece, and Rome to Spain. The bull was seen as an object of worship, as a god or as a symbol of gods; as king or a symbol of kings; and as an emblem of fertility and a victim for sacrifice. The blood or flesh of a bull given up in sacrifice was then eaten (actually or symbolically), and the eating of the flesh and drinking of the blood imparted the bull's strength and vigor. Bullfights are still popular in South America, Spain, and Portugal. In Spain, the bullfighting season begins in March and runs to October, with over a thousand bullfights in more than 350 bull rings. At least 200 ranches in Spain are entirely devoted to the breeding and rearing of fighting bulls, which go into the ring when they are between three and five years of age.

California now features bloodless bullfights, in which young matadors (matador means "the killer" in Spanish) lead charging bulls through their red capes. Unlike in Mexico or Spain, however, in California when the show ends and the animal is pierced with the spear, the spear has Velcro at the end that attaches to a patch of Velcro on the bull's back. "It's more than a sport; it's an art, it's culture," one organizer claims. "It's to control the bull and to make that into a ballet and art, and to make it do what you want it to do by using a cape."

Oxen Oracles

In the distant past, cows were felt to possess magical attributes. The Celts practiced interpretation of dreams, and in attempting to predict the future, they utilized a method of incubatory sleep that may have originated in Classical Greece, but sprung up independently within the Celtic world. Related to this method of precognitive dreaming was a mysterious ceremony known as *Tarb Feis*, or "Bull Sleep," during which a trained shaman or priest was put to sleep in a darkened hut, lying on a cured bull's hide. This strategy would produce the required trance state in the shaman from which he would emerge some hours later with words of prophecy on his lips. A similar description of this method existed as late as the seventeenth century.

More evidence of the use of cattle in divination and supernatural spells is found in the ancient use of runes, a magical primitive alphabet used by the Germanic tribes of pre-Christian Europe to ward off enemies and diseases, or to promote good health and fertility. The word *rune*, which occurs in various forms in both Germanic and Celtic languages, means "a mystery" or "a holy secret" that is "whispered," and runic inscriptions with symbols for aurochs have been found on goblets, rune-stones, and rune-staves in Sweden and Germany. The rune *Fehu* or *Feoh*, indicated "wealth in cattle." The rune *ur* or *uruz* represented the aurochs (Caesar called them *urus*), the first (wild) cows.

The Etruscans and Romans used oxen for extispicy, another form of divination, involving the "reading" of the entrails from a sacrificial ox. After removing the liver from the beast, it was used as a mirror for fifteen to twenty minutes to reflect the divine rays that the gods were thought to be continually shining down. When laid out for inspection, the oxen's intestines also revealed mystical connections, forming a spiraling labyrinth that has been depicted for millennia on stones or in clay as a sacred symbol.

In contemporary Ethiopia, the intestines of cattle are still consulted as indicators of future events by the Mursi tribe, a cattle tribe.

The bones of cattle are also used in Africa for divination purposes. Four bones, hooves, or horns from cattle are decorated with a positive and a negative side, so sixteen combinations can be formed when they are thrown on the ground. Each combination, or "fall," has a name, or "praise," the poem recited when the fall is identified. When one is learning how to become a diviner, the pupil will eventually be asked by a mentor to kill an ox from whose bones the pupil carves his or her own set of the four principal pieces. Placing the bones beneath a white ash or under white leaves on a growing tree beneath white moonlight, the pupil appeals to his or her ancestors to grant the bones the power of divination. In some tribes, the apprentice drinks a concoction of water in which the bones, plus various roots, powders, and the flesh of a white goat have been boiled, so the pupil will eventually understand "inside his heart" how to read the bones.

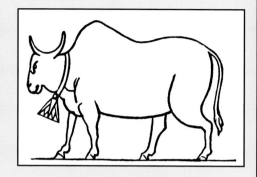

Ancient Egyptian humped ox

In Greek mythology, the Gods of Mount Olympus bestowed the art of cheese making as a gift to the human race.

Another perfect day
The familiar black-and-white Holstein has been raised in its native Holland for more than 2,000 years. (Photo © Bruce Fritz)

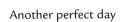

Holy Cows

Because cattle have been a part of our culture for thousands of years, almost from the beginning of time they have figured in the annals of religion, legend, and myth. As early as 19 B.C., the Roman poet Tibullus spoke of the magical use of milk: "Now with magic howlings she keeps the swarms of the grave before her: now she sprinkles them with milk and bids them retreat."

There is a legend among the Masai tribe in Kenya and Tanzania that relates that the creator, *ngai*, sent cattle to them at the beginning of time and gave them the sole right to keep them. The Masai devote their lives to their cattle, and, in turn, the cattle are responsible for the social status of tribesmen. Because of their religious belief, the Masai have cattle that vary considerably, due to the centuries-old practice of stealing cattle from neighboring tribes, sanctioned by the legend.

In fact, compared with cattle of neighboring tribes, Masai cattle are the largest and in the best condition, due largely to the generous amount of milk given to young calves. As a rule, the Masai have so many cattle that only a portion of milk is needed for human consumption and there is plenty left for the calves. For the Masai, who eat no fruit or grain, cow's milk mixed with blood is a staple food. Once a month, blood is taken from living animals by shooting a small arrow into the neck. This blood is then mixed with milk in a calabash that has been washed in urine and sterilized to prevent spoilage.

The Dun Cow: The legend of the Dun Cow of England was first mentioned in 1570, when the remains of the cow were displayed at Warwick Castle along with Sir Guy of Warwick's armor. Sir Guy of Warwick is said to have lived in Saxon times during the reign of King Athelstan. He set out from Warwick to win fame in heathen lands, and his exploits included the slaying of dragons, giants, and sultans. Perhaps his most renowned exploit was his battle with the dreaded Dun Cow at Dunsmore Heath. According to legend, the Dun Cow was a monster of a beast— said to be twelve feet high by eighteen feet long (360 cm x 540 cm)—that provided milk for many of the surrounding villages, until one day a witch decided to test the cow's powers.

The witch collected all the containers she could find and began to milk the cow into a sieve, catching the milk in the containers. Occasionally the cow glanced back, but noticing that the sieve remained empty, she continued to give her milk. Soon all the containers were full. Neighbors arrived and filled their containers in a similar manner. The cow kept giving milk because the sieve still appeared empty! By dusk, a great line of men and women waited patiently for their turn to milk the Dun Cow, and it seemed that as long as the sieve appeared empty, there would be milk enough for all. But as darkness gathered and the last few village folk awaited their turn, the cow gazed down and realized she had been tricked. Upon discovery of the fraud, the cow is supposed to have gone mad and to have terrorized Dunsmore Heath and surrounding villages for months on end, causing people to leave their homes.

At last, Guy, Earl of Warwick, armed with a strong battleaxe, bow, and quiver, came to the rescue. He attacked the dreaded Dun Cow, and the beast died under a welter of blows after a fierce struggle. The King summoned Guy to York, presented him with a feast, gave him a Knighthood, and a rib from the Dun Cow was hung with due ceremony in Warwick Castle. Today, the castle displays something like a huge tusk, supposed to be one of the horns. The famed Dun Cow has appeared as an apparition to the Earl of Warwick before the death of a family member. Her hooves are silent, and she leaves no traces of her hoofprints on the grass.

Celtic Saints: Saints Brigid, Naile, Patrick, and Kevin experienced unusual incidents with cows, contributing to their sainthood. Saint Brigid's mother was a maid. At sunrise when the pregnant woman crossed over the threshold of the house with a pitcher of milk in her hand, she went into labor. The baby, Brigid, was washed with the milk that was still in her mother's hand. Unfortunately, Brigid's father was a wizard, and from birth, the child was destined to such a degree of holiness that she vomited up all unclean food. When her wizard father observed this, he entrusted a particular red-eared cow to give milk only to Brigid, and he let a faithful woman milk this cow; the holy child did not throw up the special milk.

Saint Naile's mother had a dream before he was born that she gave birth to a dog that was washed in milk. When she awoke, she told her dream to her husband whose interpretation was that she would give birth to a son who would fill Ireland with his piety and learning.

During the period that Saint Patrick was held captive, he was kept busy herding cattle; his duty was to keep the calves away from the cows. This was apparently a duty of many Irish saints during their childhood, and it provided the setting for a favorite miracle: The youth took his staff and drew a line upon the ground between the calves and the cows that neither would cross, thus leaving the saint free to give his or her undivided attention to study or heavenly contemplation.

Saint Kevin visited a hermit who possessed only one cow. He was asked to watch the cow for a day, because the hermit's servant was busy. During the day, the cow gave birth to a calf, but Kevin took pity on a starving wolf and fed the calf to the wolf. The frantic cow ran to the hermit, who reproached Kevin for what he had done. Kevin went back to the woods, called the wolf, and in the name of Christ commanded that the wolf take the place of the calf by standing next to the cow during every milking; this followed an Irish belief to help the cow's milk come down. Each day at milking time, the wolf emerged from the woods and stood in front of the cow who licked it and dutifully let down her milk.

Saint Martin: The Patron Saint of France is honored on Martinmas, or St. Martin's Day, November 11. Also known as St. Martin of Tours, he is famous for his generosity. According to legend, one cold day, Martin encountered a nearly naked beggar. He used his sword to split his own cloak, giving part to the needy man.

That night during his sleep Martin was visited by Christ dressed in the half of the garment he had given away.

No one knows how or why the British custom of slaughtering cattle on St. Martin's Day evolved, but Martinmas is related to the derivation of the word *free-martin* for a sterile female calf. Usually only one calf is produced during the nine-month period of gestation in cattle, but, occasionally, twins are born, and when these are of both sexes, the female is almost invariably sterile. In England, such an animal was called a *free-martin,* meaning "a cow free for fattening." *Mart,* an old provincial English and Scottish abbreviation of *Martinmas,* meant a beef or other animal slaughtered at Martinmas, the celebration that took the place of an old pagan festival.

Archangel Michael: In Estonia, Michaelmas Day, or the Archangel Michael's name day, marks the end of the summer. According to custom, a sheep is killed, beer is brewed, and harvest festivals are celebrated. This has traditionally been the time when contracts for farmhands hired for the summer months are concluded. Michaelmas bonfires light the hillsides, and in the evening when cattle came home from the pasture, they are watched to be sure there are no telltale traces of grass in their mouths, an omen of shortage of food for the winter. It was also once believed that after Michaelmas, wolves had permission to kill domestic animals, so cattle were no longer left outside for the night.

Hogmanay: The Scottish New Year celebration Hogmanay has become renowned for the effusive manner in which the new year is greeted, but the most im-

portant element is the belief that the new year must begin on a happy note. Still celebrated in the Scottish Highlands, Hogmanay tradition has children go door to door asking for presents. In the early days of this celebration, a curious custom prevailed: The people of the area assembled, and the stoutest of the party was presented with a dried cow hide that he dragged behind him while the rest followed, beating the hide with sticks and singing.

After going around the house three times, each person recited another rhyme that extolled the hospitality of the master and the mistress, and the visitors were regaled with bread and butter, cheese and whiskey. Before leaving, one of the group would burn the breast part of a sheepskin and put it to the nose of everyone present, as a charm against witchcraft and infection.

Ludmila: The patron saint of dairymaids, or *Die Heilige Notburga*, Ludmila is a legendary character in the tiny principality of Liechtenstein. Each fall, when the cows come back down from the mountains where they have spent the summer under the watchful eyes of herdsmen, the best cow of the summer leads the procession from the high pastures with a one-legged milking stool attached between her horns, beribboned with garlands of flowers and colorful streamers, and a wreath of laurel leaves around her head. Ludmila was a fourteenth-century milkmaid who, because of her piety, faith, and devotion to the Virgin Mary, became a saint devoted to the care of Alpine cattle and their herdsmen. A weakling cow under her care in 1823 produced a miracle that created the enduring story.

Good Breeding

Some things in especial measure breathe the romance and poetry and magic of life on the land. Such are rows of weather-beaten droning beehives under gnarled and apple trees, and running streams with cows standing knee deep in clear pools and long shady lanes with many beaten cow-paths, and boys calling the cows when the sun is low, and sunken mossy stone walls, and these last are the best and richest.
—Jared Van Wagenen, Jr.,
The Cow, 1922

Contented Ayrshires
Facing page: An Ayrshire herd takes it easy.
(Photo © David Lorenz Winston)

"Heavy Shorthorn Grade Cattle"
Right: Shorthorn cattle, as illustrated in this engraving from the *American Agriculturalist* from December 1874, were originally called Durhams, and came from the counties of Durham, Northumberland, Lincoln, and York on the northeastern coast of England. The Tees River runs through this area and the breed was also referred to as Teeswater cattle. One story claims that when William, Prince of Orange, took the British throne, he so missed the creamy milk from his native Dutch cattle that he had a shipload of them imported to England, and this was perhaps the first improvement of native English cattle.

Say "cow" to most people, and it will probably inspire the image of the familiar black-and-white dairy cow, the Holstein. But what if you're in South Africa, where *cow* is referred to by a word that sounds like *Koei*, or in China, where cow is pronounced *Nui*?

Hpw to Say Cow in Fourteen Countries

Denmark: *Koe*

Estonia: *Lehm*

Finland: *Lehmä*

France: *Vache*

Germany: *Kuh*

Indonesia: *Sapi*

Italy: *Vacca* or *Mucca*

Japan: *Ushi*

Korea: *So*

Poland: *Krowa*

Russia: *Korova*

Serbia: *Crava*

Spain: *Vaca*

Sweden: *Ko*

Although we have six major dairy breeds in North America (Guernsey, Jersey, Milking Shorthorn, Ayrshire, Holstein, and Brown Swiss) and even more beef breeds (Angus, Polled Hereford, Limousin, Charolais, Simmental, Maine-Anjou, Salers, Pinzgauer, Gelbvieh, and others), there are actually more than a thousand different breeds of domesticated cattle around the world, in all shapes and sizes with astonishing variety.

Spotted, dappled roan, brindle—cattle on our planet range from the pure White Park to Belgian Blue to solid Black Angus and shades of gray, red, and yellow in between. The Highland cattle of Scotland have long curls and shaggy forelocks, while the Santander Hairless in Colombia, South America, are almost bald. You can find cows with short, stumpy horns, cows boasting gigantic and graceful horns, or cows that are born naturally polled, without any horns at all. There are cute little miniature cattle, whopping gigantic cattle, cattle with smooth withers or shouldering flopping humps of muscle and fat, and cattle who graze in lush Alpine pastures or adapt to scanty forage on parched, arid plains.

The Aurochs

All cattle are of one species, descended from the wild aurochs, *Bos primigenius*. Aurochs are best known today from portraits and engravings found on cave walls near Lascaux, in southwest France. But additional cave paintings discovered in Abrigo de los Toros, the "Cave of the Bulls," in Spain, and skeletons unearthed in Turkey and North Africa reveal that as far back as 6500 B.C., domesticated cattle were providing milk and meat to early humans. Bones found in caves in Scotland indicate that *Bos primigenius* was hunted by early settlers there; remains have also been unearthed in the marl

Aurochs woodcut

This woodcut of an aurochs appeared in Edward Topsell's *History of Four-footed Beasts and Serpents* from 1658. In his book, the Reverend Topsell says of the bull: "His noble courage is in his looke and in his frowning countenance or forhead." Topsell also claimed that, "If one make a small candle of paper and cow's marrow and setting the same on fire under his browse or eyelids which are balde, without haire, and often annoynting the place, he shall have very decent and comely haire grow thereupon."

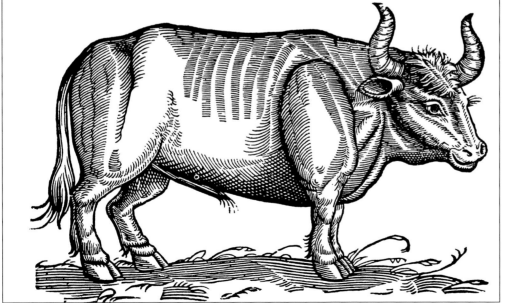

deposits of Wigtonshire and Caithness, Scotland. Fossilized bones have turned up in the lower kitchen debris of early lake dwellers in Great Britain, Italy, Switzerland, and Germany. All of this evidence helps to give us a clear image of the aurochs, the bovine ancestor whose initial origins can be traced to the subcontinent of India.

After the Great Ice Age (250,000 years ago) the aurochsen spread from western Asia eastward to China and westward to the Middle East, then to northern Africa and Europe during the Pleistocene period, but none of the aurochs ever reached the American continent, Australia, or New Zealand.

When aurochs began their journey around the globe as companions to migrating human tribes, they began to differentiate according to the regional environments and the needs of the tribes they accompanied.

Cattle are of the genus *Bos*, which encompasses ruminant quadrupeds, including wild and domesticated cattle, distinguished by a stout body and hollow, curved horns that stand out laterally from the skull. Originally there were three geographical races of aurochs: *Bos primigenius primigenius* in Europe, *Bos primigenius namadicus* in Asia, and *Bos primigenius* in North Africa. Essentially they were similar, varying only in body size and horn shape. Two major types or subspecies of aurochs eventually developed: the *Bos primigenius primigenius*, which became the European ancestor of today's humpless cattle (like the Holstein, Angus and Brown Swiss), and the *Bos primigenius namadicus*, which was the Asiatic form that became the direct ancestor of the zebu, or the humped cattle

(such as the Brahman).

Aurochsen were gargantuan animals with dangerous lyre-shaped horns and long legs. The cows had small udders, and cows and calves were reddish brown. The bulls, which measured as much as six feet tall (180 cm) at the withers, were black with pale dorsal stripes and had white curly hair between the horns and white muzzle rings. The largest known aurochs skull, found in Rome, had horn cores with a circumference of 19.6 inches (50 cm) at the base.

The Emperor Charlemagne hunted the wild aurochs in the forests near Aix-La-Chapelle, France, in the ninth century. In 1556, the imperial German envoy Freiherr von Herberstain wrote of the aurochs, or urochs, claiming "Girdles from the leather of the urochs are highly prized and are worn by ladies. The Queen of Poland presented me with twain thereof, and the Roman Queen very graciously accepted one of these." Tacitus and Pliny wrote that the horns of these cattle, used as drinking cups, sometimes held as much as two urs, or about two quarts (approximately two liters).

Julius Caesar, in his chronicle of the *Gallic War* (VI, 28) called the aurochs *urus,* and said they were native in the Black Forest of Germany. In 65 B.C., Caesar explained, "There is a third kind of these animals which are called uri. In size these are but little inferior to elephants, although in appearance, colour and form, they are bulls. Their strength and their speed are great. They spare neither men nor beast when they see them. In the expanse of their horns, as well as in form and appearance, they differ much from our oxen." Caesar was also convinced that the urus had no joints in its legs, and

Aurochs de Heck
Descendents of the Heck brothers' experiments to recreate the aurochs, these Aurochs de Heck are found in game farms and zoological parks in western Europe. The French organization *Syndikat International pour l'Elevage la Réintroduction et le Développement de l'Aurochs de Heck* (SIERDAH) was created to further the preservation and promotion of the Heck-Aurochs as a separate breed. (Photo © Claude Guintard, SIERDAH)

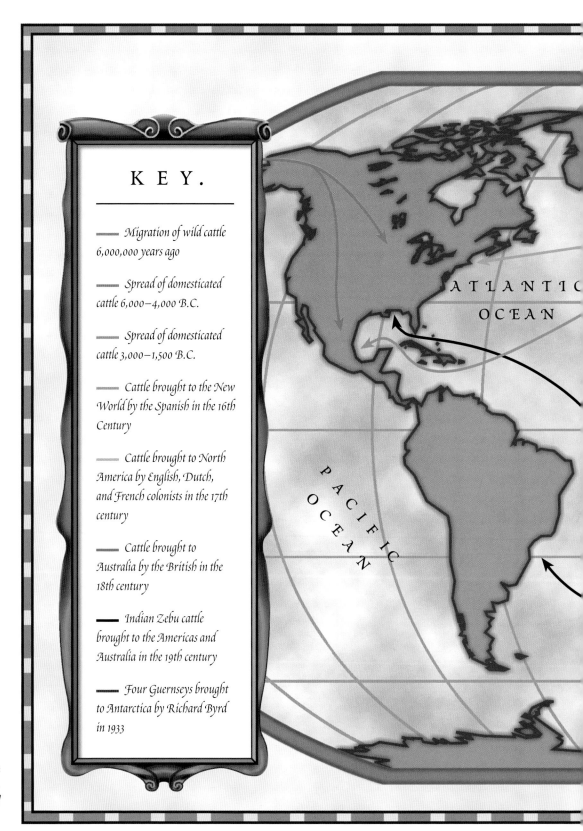

KEY.

—— *Migration of wild cattle 6,000,000 years ago*

•••••• *Spread of domesticated cattle 6,000–4,000 B.C.*

—— *Spread of domesticated cattle 3,000–1,500 B.C.*

—— *Cattle brought to the New World by the Spanish in the 16th Century*

—— *Cattle brought to North America by English, Dutch, and French colonists in the 17th century*

—— *Cattle brought to Australia by the British in the 18th century*

—— *Indian Zebu cattle brought to the Americas and Australia in the 19th century*

—— *Four Guernseys brought to Antarctica by Richard Byrd in 1933*

ATLANTIC OCEAN

PACIFIC OCEAN

Cow migration
This map tracks the migration of cattle throughout history and throughout the world. The map was adapted from *Cattle of the World* by John Friend and Dennis Bishop.

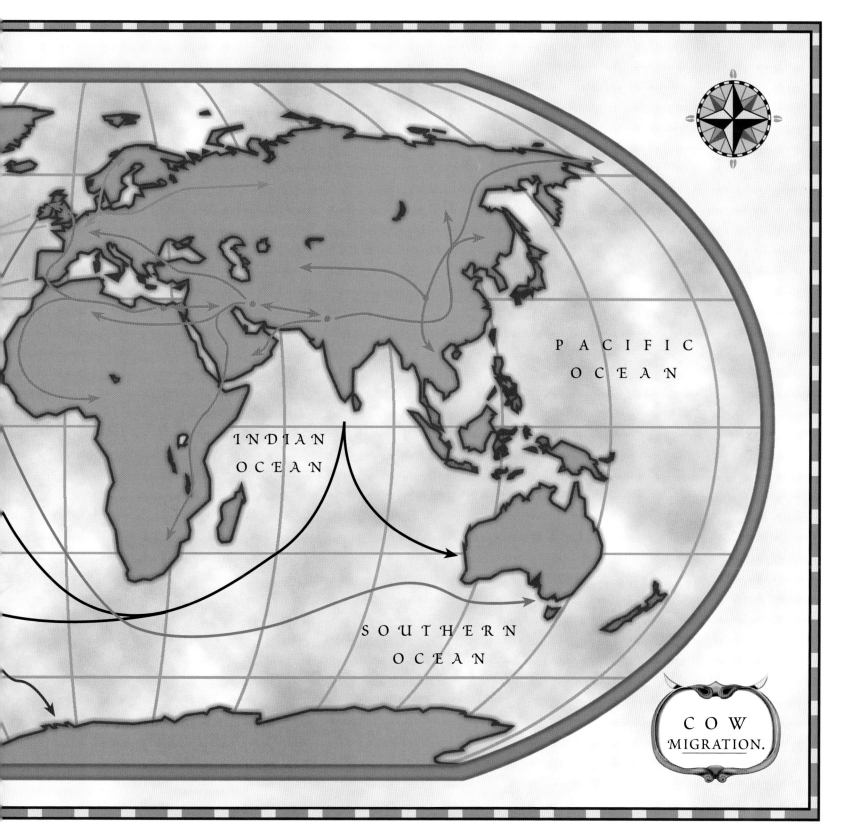

PACIFIC
OCEAN

INDIAN
OCEAN

SOUTHERN
OCEAN

COW
MIGRATION.

Aurochs hunt

This woodcut depicts a sixteenth-century French hunter using a tree as a shield while he spears a charging aurochs.

described a means of hunting them that sounds suspiciously like cow-tipping: Aurochsen were known to lean against trees when they slept, so hunters would cut a deep gash into the tree. When an aurochs was tired and leaned against the tree, the slashed tree would break, the aurochs would fall and could not rise again.

European aurochsen outlived the other strains, and although the aurochs had been captured in words by Julius Caesar in 65 B.C., its portrait had been gloriously immortalized in Greek and Roman mythologies, and its hide supremely girdled a Roman Queen, the last known wild aurochs cow—the final ancestral link to every bovine creature currently on the face of this earth—died in 1627 when it was shot in Jaktorowka, a remote game preserve for noblemen south of Warsaw, Poland.

Three centuries later, Dr. Lutz Heck,

director of the Berlin Zoo, wished to experiment with back-breeding an animal that resembled the extinct aurochs. Heck had been fascinated with aurochs since his youth when he read of their presence in medieval European game reserves. In the 1920s, Heck began crossbreeding semiferal Camargue cattle and Andalucian fighting bulls, to "breed back" the aurochs. Meanwhile, his brother, Heinz Heck, was trying to recreate aurochsen at the Hellabrunn Zoological Gardens in Munich. In contrast to Lutz's careful breeding scheme, Heinz bred Corsican cattle with Highlands from Scotland, various Alpine breeds, Hungarian and Podolian Steppe cattle, and Friesians, all thrown together. After twenty-five years of effort, Lutz ended up with reddish heifers and black bulls with white muzzles and light brown dorsal stripes. Heinz developed a reddish heifer and a black bull with a white muzzle and a white or pale yellow dorsal stripe.

The Heck brothers were elated and felt they were successful in recreating the aurochs. In 1952, Lutz Heck rejoiced in the results in *Animals, My Adventure*: "These cattle I crossed on a definite, carefully considered plan, and with the patience of the breeder I eliminated the unwanted elements again and again, through years of effort. In the years that followed, over a hundred calves saw the light of day. And then my brother and I both had the same experience: suddenly, to our surprise, there appeared a calf corresponding entirely to the wild form and also developing in correspondence with it. And after a further period of years we were in possession of stocks with a quite stable heritable constitution . . . and anyone who surveys the result achieved, the fine group of aurochsen and their splendid dark stud-bulls, with the genuine ancestral markings, the reddish line along the back, and who sees the red-coloured cows and the grey calves, must admit that the experiment has succeeded. The aurochs has been brought back into existence."

Geneticists remain skeptical of the Heck brothers' aurochsen (now known as Heck-ochs or Heck-Aurochs), but approximately 150 descendants of the Munich breed thrive. Many are visible to the public at zoological parks and game farms in western Europe, such as the Bergerie Nationale in Rambouillet, the Ferme de l'Aurochs in Jura, and the Zoorama Européen de Chize, all in France; and the Park Animalier de Han-Sur Lesse in Belgium, and the Parc Animalier de Neanderthal in Germany. Beef from the Heck-ochs/Aurochs are served at premier restaurants in Paris, where "nature beef" is valued for its organic and emotional origins.

The Concept of "Breed"

A "breed" is a group of animals that, through selection and breeding, have come to resemble one another and pass those traits uniformly to their offspring. This gets more complicated when you have a crossbred animal that is actually a composite of several other breeds which is then awarded a breed name of its own, like Santa Gertrudis, Beefmaster, Brangus, Braford, Beefalo, or RX3.

Some of the new composite breeds have been created by the selection of particular traits that give them special purpose. The RX3 is a synthesis of three red American breeds: the Hereford, Red and White Holsteins, and pure Red Angus.

Other breeds have been perfected within the breed (Holstein, for example) to enhance their natural traits—Holsteins are high-producing milkers. And then there are breeds whose traits may have developed naturally as a result of the environment in which they were developed, like the N'Dama in East Africa that has developed a resistance to diseases spread by the tse-tse fly, fatal to most breeds of cattle but not the N'Dama, which has built up an immunity, or trypanotolerance, through the years. And in India, where cattle are sacred and live in the streets, breeds such as the Nelore are neither slaughtered nor managed for reproduction, and the genetic selection has always been a natural process, favoring the survival of the strongest and best prepared to withstand the heat, the lack of forage, the prolonged dry season, and the many diseases.

Our earliest ancestors may have favored animals with unusual coat color, patterns, or horn shapes because these traits kept them identifiable as distinct from the wild stock. But, just as cows seem to appeal to us because they represent the essence of motherhood, it is probable that cattle were initially domesticated not to supply milk or meat, but for use as sacrificial animals in fertility rites honoring the lunar mother-goddess: the lyre-shaped horns were reminiscent of the crescent moon.

Then there were the Battle-Axe people of Central Europe and the Celts who associated the various colors of cattle with the worship of pagan spirits: Black animals embodied pestilence and death; red animals represented fertility and crops; white animals symbolized worship of the sun.

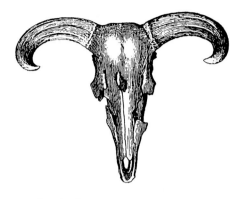

Aurochs skull
Illustration of an aurochs skull found during an archaeological excavation in Great Britain.

A cow's heart weighs about five pounds (2.25 kg) and pumps 400 pints (188 liters) of blood through the udder to produce one pint (.5 liters) of milk. That means nearly 10,000 pints (4,700 liters) of blood are pumped through a cow's udder daily to produce three gallons (114 liters) of milk.

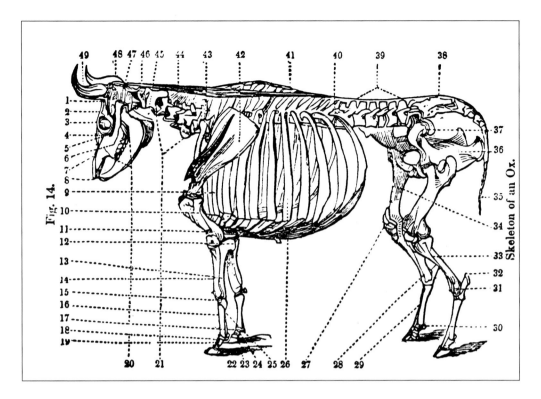

Fig. 14.   Skeleton of an Ox.

Bovine skeleton

This illustration from a farming handbook of the 1880s outlines a bovine skeleton.

A cow has about 207 bones
in its body.

Or particular cattle may have been selected for entertainment purposes, as animals have been used for sport since the earliest civilizations. The Cretan sport of bull-leaping in the second millennium B.C. was a precursor of the more brutal spectacle of the Roman amphitheater, or present-day bullfighting in Spain and Mexico.

Until the mid-eighteenth century in Britain, agricultural prizes were awarded to cattle for their long legs, important for oxen that must tramp through undrained lowlands and narrow lanes in the mire. An old Scottish superstition suggested that white cows gave inferior milk, so red cows were preferred in that country. In old English medical books, when milk was ordered to be given to a patient it was frequently specified that it should be taken from a red cow.

In selecting animals for such a vari-

ety of personal needs, however, we may have purposely enhanced traits that in the process caused the domesticated stock to be less fit or able to exist without our protection, as they lost size, camouflage, instinct, brain capacity, and sometimes the courage to defend themselves.

In most early developing cultures, sheep and goats were milked instead of cows. Cattle were more likely to be utilized for their muscle power, to aid in cultivation, to draw carts and heavy timber, or to carry packs or people on their backs. Humped cattle, or zebu, are believed to have been first domesticated anywhere from 2100 B.C. to 4000 B.C. Marco Polo (1254–1324) exuberantly described the humped oxen of Persia by writing, "They are very large, and all over white as snow, the hair is very short and smooth, which is owing to the heat of the country. The horns are short and thick, not sharp in the point; and between the shoulders they have a hump some two palms high. There are no handsomer creatures in the world. When they have to be loaded they kneel like the camel; once the load is adjusted, they rise. Their load is a heavy one, for they are very strong animals."

Even today, despite the gradual mechanization of agriculture and transportation, oxen are necessary for subsistence-level farming. Such animals are only eaten when they are no longer fit for work, if they are eaten at all, and milked for the household only after the calves have had their fill.

The evolution of beef cattle from such heavily muscled bovines seems obvious. The development of milk cows, however, occurred only relatively recently,

Cows have cloven hooves, *Prose and Poetry of the Livestock Industry* (1905) claims, and "In galloping through boggy places or in deep mud, cattle can distance a horse. Their toes spread, and therefore their wide feet do not sink so deep as do those of the solid-hoofed horse. Furthermore, the cleft between the toes permits the air to enter the hole in the mud as the foot is raised; whereas the horse must overcome a partial vacuum when it withdraws its hoof, and so wastes considerable muscular effort beside having its speed retarded and its self-confidence shaken."

Brown Swiss cow in the Swiss Alps
The beautiful Brown Swiss is one of the oldest of the world's dairy breeds, descended from cattle used in the mountains and valleys of Switzerland before recorded history. Evidence has been found that a type of cattle closely related to the breed once existed in Switzerland, as far back as the Bronze Age. (Photo © Lynn M. Stone)

of central Europe were recognized as a source of excellent beef.

Amazingly, a formal concept of "breeds" did not exist until the last two centuries, and the man given credit for imposing structure on the principle of "like-breeds-like," was English agriculturist Robert Bakewell (1725–1795). Bakewell began his experiments in 1755 with Longhorned cattle (no relation to the Texas Longhorn) native to central England. The British Longhorns were short-lived, however, and toward the end of Queen Victoria's reign, the breed was considered to be in decline. A Victorian writer remarked, "Although we look upon them with a kindly historic interest, it must now be reluctantly admitted that there is little reason for their continued existence."

Students of Bakewell carried out similar inbreeding and controlled selection in the late 1700s, with much more lasting success. Robert and Charles Colling, using Bakewell's principles of inbreeding, developed the first systematic breeding program on cattle then known as the "Teeswater breed." In 1805, a bull called Comet, calved from the Collings' breeding system, caused a sensation when he sold for a fantastic sum at public auction. The first herd book of any breed of cattle was founded in 1822 by George Coates. In 1874, the Coates Herd Book was acquired by the Shorthorn Society of Great Britain and Ireland, as the association and the herd book gave great credibility to the breed.

Shorthorns (also referred to as Durham) were introduced to North America

"The Good Milker"
Farming how-to books flourished in North America in the late 1800s and early 1900s, chock full of advice on everything from beef cattle breeds to "milch" cows. (Photo © Keith Baum)

and a pattern of selective breeding eventually developed. The greatest variety of cattle breeds came about in France, Germany, Italy, and the United Kingdom. There, each breed evolved and usually took its name from the area in which it was developed. Without a network of interconnecting roads, most of these breeds were able to exist in relative isolation, undisturbed by genetic influences from other locales. Specialized milk cows happened to be bred in the lowlands of northern Europe, dual-purpose (milk and beef) breeds became established in Europe as a whole, and the big draft cattle

as early as 1783. They were valued by early settlers for their milk and meat, as well as for their willing power for the wagon and the plow. The American Shorthorn Herd Book, begun in 1846, was the first to be published in the United States for any breed.

Toward the end of the eighteenth century, horses began to replace oxen in the fields and on the road. Agricultural improvements provided good winter forage to fatten meat animals, and urbanization and the Industrial Revolution created an enormous consumer demand for food, with an effect on cattle breeding. For example, in the second half of the eighteenth century, every Londoner purchased an average of half a pound (0.225 kg) of meat a day—more than twice as much as the average in Paris or Brussels. There was a considerable exodus from countryside to town in the new industrial age, and people required both meat and milk. There was also a heavy demand for tallow for candles; thus the animals (sheep as well as cattle) became much fatter. This era also saw a rapid change from all-purpose, subsistence-farm animals to commercial herds that were able to supply milk and meat for those who had no access to land to produce their own.

A golden age of cattle breeding occurred during the nineteenth century, bringing about the prominence of Hereford, Aberdeen-Angus, Holstein, Guernsey, Brown Swiss, and others that are still highly regarded today as premier breeds, and driving other breeds to extinction when the twentieth century dawned. In 1900, western Europe had about 230 native breeds of cattle. By 1988, only about thirty of these breeds were stable; seventy

Cow stomachs
Right, top: The cow possesses four stomachs with a total capacity of thirty-five gallons (105 liters). The first stomach is called the *Rumen*, or paunch. The second stomach is the *Reticulum*. The third stomach is the *Omasum* or *"manyplies."* The fourth stomach is called the *Abomasum*. The Rumen is where food goes when the cow swallows the first time. Cows don't chew much before they swallow, so this first stomach softens things up a bit; then the wad is regurgitated to be chewed as *cud*, and swallowed a second time when it goes directly to the second stomach, and so on.

Livestock advertisement, circa 1880s
Right, bottom: "Cow towns," such as Kansas City, Missouri, saw their origin as a result of the early cattle drives. For a long time, the area around the Flint Hills was controlled by Texas cattle ranchers who used the grassy land to build up their herds after long drives north to the railroads, where the cattle were shipped east for fattening and slaughter.

had become extinct, and fifty-three were in an endangered state. The remainder were minority breeds, not immediately endangered, but far from secure. Yet, amazingly, a tremendous diversity of domestic cattle still exist on this planet.

The Global Barnyard:
European Breeds

As far back in history as 60 B.C., the Roman agricultural writer Columella de-

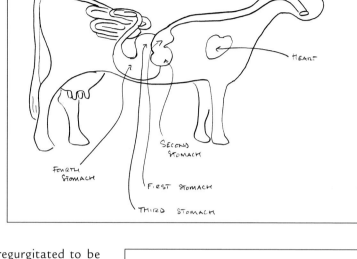

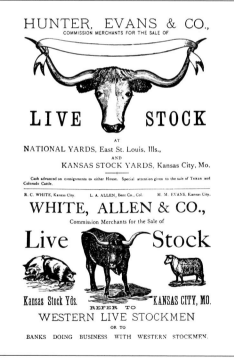

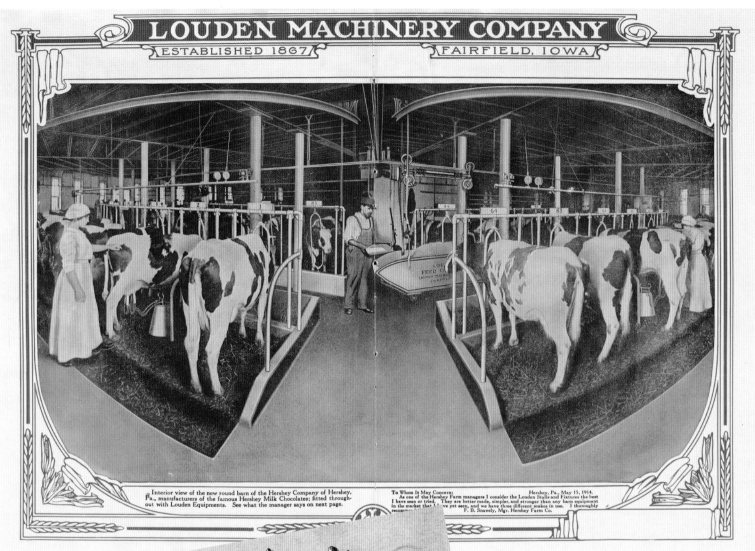

LOUDEN MACHINERY COMPANY
ESTABLISHED 1867 — FAIRFIELD, IOWA

Interior view of the new round barn of the Hershey Company of Hershey, Pa., manufacturers of the famous Hershey Milk Chocolates; fitted throughout with Louden Equipments. See what the manager says on next page.

To Whom It May Concern: Hershey, Pa., May 15, 1914.
As one of the Hershey Farm managers I consider the Louden Stalls and Fixtures the best I have seen or tried. They are better made, simpler, and stronger than any barn equipment in the market that I have yet seen, and we have three different makes in use. I thoroughly recommend them.
F. B. Snavely, Mgr. Hershey Farm Co.

Hershey's chocolate label and bovine workers
A crucial use for cow's milk is milk chocolate. As this vintage chocolate bar label promises, "Hershey's Chocolate for breakfast, lunch and dinner." Providing milk for the chocolate was the aim of this herd of cows at work in Hershey's round barn in Hershey, Pennsylvania, as pictured in a Louden Machinery Company catalog from 1917.

scribed a variety of cattle of that period and how they differed in conformation, disposition, and coat colors according to the place and the climate in which they lived. The United Kingdom, The Netherlands, France, Germany, and Italy were home to a large number of popular breeds, many of which have been exported and are now in existence throughout the world. The Holstein, from the Netherlands, was originally known there as the Dutch Black Pied, or Dutch Black and White, and gained other names when it was exported to other countries, as was the black-and-white Friesian. Growing in popularity in the United States, but now rare in its home country, is the black-and-white Dutch Belted, or Lakenvelder.

Traditionally, the cattle of Europe were used for milk, meat, and muscle. The Limousin of France, originally used for draft, is now widely exported internationally. Other beef breeds now enjoying a widespread influence include the Blonde D'Aquitaine, Aubrac, Salers, Charolais, Tarentaise, Belgian Blue, and Parthenais. The French dairy breeds were found in the northern part of France, where the Normande still flourishes today.

Spanish breeds are familiar to fans of Hollywood westerns, for Spanish and Portuguese cattle were the foundations of the Texas Longhorn and the Criollos in Latin America. The Ganado Bravo or Toro de Lidia, famous fighting bulls, are selectively bred in both countries.

There are three general groups of indigenous cattle in Italy, identified by geography and genetic features. The Pinzgauer is representative of the mountain breeds; it is a dual-purpose animal. The Podolian breeds are similar to the Grey Steppe cattle of eastern Europe, originally valued for work and for meat; the Chianina, Romagnola, Marchigiana, and Maremmana are characteristic of these cattle. Of the plains breeds, the Reggiana is known for the *parmigiano reggiano*, or parmesan cheese made from its milk. The Piedmont, or Piemontese, is now gaining popularity in the United States.

Switzerland, Austria, and the German Alps have produced fine dairy and beef cattle for centuries. Austria is famous for its Simmental and Pinzgauer breeds. Brown Swiss, or Braunvieh, had their origins in Switzerland. The Gelbvieh, a beef breed from Germany, was bred in the 1870s when a uniformity of yellow-brown color, capacity for work, and growth potential were sought. Since World War II, many German breeds have become extinct: In nineteenth century Bavaria, for instance, there were thirty-five cattle breeds, where today there are only five. A variety of breeds in many

Cows at Stonehenge
Since the Druids reportedly used cattle in sacrificial ceremonies, it would not seem all that unusual to see cows at Stonehenge, a megalithic site on Salisbury Plain in Wiltshire, west of Amesbury, England, whose mysterious stone circles date back to the eighth or ninth millennium B.C. However, contrary to popular belief, the Druids bear no actual historical connection with Stonehenge. It is also doubtful, as Geoffrey of Monmouth stated in 1135, that Stonehenge was carried by a tribe of giants from Africa to Ireland and then flown by the wizard Merlin across the sea. (Photo © David Lorenz Winston)

British Longhorn and calf

The British Longhorn played a significant role in the "like-breeds-like" experiments of English agriculturist Robert Bakewell in 1725–1795. Currently it is considered a "vulnerable" breed, with approximately 450 breeding cows surviving. (Photo © Lynn Stone)

Hinterwalder cow

The Hinterwald, or *Hinterwälder Rind*, survived a century-long process of selection in the mountains of the Black Forest, and is a sure-footed, fine-featured, undemanding cow. Today, the Hinterwald is the smallest cattle breed in central Europe, and is an endangered breed. Several Swiss organizations have set up programs to help maintain the Hinterwald, directing a breeding program and maintaining a herd book. (Photo © Lynn Stone)

A cow will eat about 100 pounds (45 kg) of grass daily.

eastern European countries suffered a similar fate.

The Belarus Red, also known as White-Russian Red (or Krasnaya belorusskaya), is the result of crossbreeding with German, Danish, Polish, Estonian, and Latvian red and brown cattle. It was developed at the Vasilishkovskaya Animal Husbandry Experiment Station, and the cattle are found in all regions of Belarus, but are most common in Grodno and Minsk.

Great Britain, somewhat isolated geographically from the rest of Europe, is able to document the domestication of cattle in that country as far back as Neolithic times, and succeeding invasions by Romans and Vikings had an effect on the development of British breeds. Indigenous to Britain are the familiar

Aberdeen-Angus, Ayrshire, Hereford, Shorthorn, Jersey, and Guernsey, as well as the Galloway, Irish Moiled, British White, Highland, Luing, Devon, Sussex, White Park, Kerry, and Dexter.

Scandinavian countries have recently attempted to create uniform national breeds by mingling the characteristics in indigenous stock. Norway's national dairy breed, the Norwegian Red, for example, was formed in the 1960s by the amalgamation of several red or red-and-white types. Some small, local Celtic-type cattle still inhabit Iceland, but the Swedish Red-and-White is another composite breed, and the Finnish Ayrshire represents about 80 percent of Finland's herds.

Asian Breeds

If you include 5 million yak and 145 million water buffalo, the cattle of Asia outnumber those of all other continents except the Americas. The domestic bovine population of Asia totals more than 500 million animals.

Cattle are the most important and most numerous livestock in the subcontinent of India and Pakistan. All the indigenous cattle of these countries are of the zebu type, with long faces, prominent humps, large drooping ears, slim legs, generous dewlaps, and upright horns. Respect for cattle, due to religion or economy, has encouraged the development of distinct breeds in these countries, as contrasted with Nepal, for example, where zebu have been crossed with the yak. Several breeds have been exported with success to other countries: The Gir has been exported to Australia, North and South America; the Sahiwal and Red Sindhi have become important breeds in Australia and Africa.

The famous Kobe beef was originally developed in Japan from virgin Wagyu heifers. The term "Wagyu" refers to native Japanese cattle, as opposed to imported breeds. The predominant national breed, the Japanese Black, has been improved through the years with the addition of European breeds. Today, the demand for high-quality beef in Japan must be met with imported animals, primarily from Australia. Purebred North American Holsteins are the dominant dairy breed.

With one-fifteenth of the world's land mass, China's regional climates and topography encourage a variety of environments and cattle breeds, including nearly 700,000 specially bred dairy cattle like the Chinese Black-and-White. The Dulong, for example, is a strange-appearing breed. Captured by hunters in the northwest of Yunnan Province, these cattle feed on bamboo, reeds, and weeds, and graze year-round in the mountains. They have a larger body size than the local cattle and their chromosome number differs from those of *Bos taurus* or the wild cattle, *Bos gaurus*, so the Dulong is considered another cattle species: *Bos frontalis*.

A Yakow is a crossbred yak-and-cow combination, common and traditional in regions such as Tibet, where the domesticated yak is found. Although the males are sterile, the females are fertile and have

A cow doesn't bite the grass that feeds her; instead, she curls her tongue around it.

Augeronne
An 1860 illustration of an Augeronne cow, one of several French breeds of cattle that became the foundation for the current Normande breed.

daily milk yields double those of the yak and greater than local zebu cows.

The best non-European dairy breed is considered to be the Damascus, the most productive dairy breed in the Middle East. The cattle are raised with meticulous care, given supplemental feed, and housed inside at night and during the rainy season.

African Breeds

The giant horned wild oxen of the Nile Valley were some of the first domesticated cattle on this continent. Their descendants include the Kuri of West Africa, the Ankole and N'Guni of East Africa, and the Nilotic cattle of the Sudan.

The main cattle country is the relatively dry area of West Africa, and Nigeria is a primary source of African cattle. Found in the Ovamboland reserve, the diminutive Ovambo cattle owe their small size to a lack of phosphorous in the soil. The Ovambo are docile, and are managed by caring herdsmen who run them between grasslands and watering places, enclosing them in corrals at night. The calves are kept with their mothers, and the cows are rarely milked. Most Ovambo cattle die of old age, but on ceremonial occasions the poorest specimens may be slaughtered. An exception is the chieftain's prize ox, the living symbol of the highest tribal status. The chief's ox is slaughtered only when the chieftain dies.

Because of the prevalence of insects in Africa, cattle have had to adapt environmentally. The N'Dama of the northern Sierra Leone are trypanotolerant, or resistant to diseases carried by the tse-tse fly, and typical of the small humpless cattle of West Africa. Sanga, or zebu cattle, first evolved in East Africa, and today the cattle breeds found in this part of the world are predominantly zebu, similar to those of India. This is also the home of the Ankole, with its remarkable horns. Each tribe has developed its own Ankole (such as the Ankole-Watusi) from the basic red, fawn, brown, and pied patterns, and the horns that distinguish them are a source of tribal pride.

The strongest beef breed in South Africa is the Bonsmara, named for Bonsma, the man who played a major role in the development of the breed, and Mara, the experimental farm where the animals were bred by the Department of Agriculture. South Africa's cattle population also includes the Drakensberger, N'Guni, and Bapedi, besides other imported herds of Shorthorns, Santa Gertrudis, Brown Swiss, and Friesland—which has the same Dutch origins as the Holstein and the Holstein-Friesian.

The Africander breed, which began in South Africa, is now also found in Australia. Huge herds of Africanders were owned by the Hottentots in 1652 when the Dutch established the Cape Colony. Colonists used the animals as oxen to pull the Boer farmers and their families on the Great Trek of 1835–1836 from the Cape of Good Hope to the Orange Free State, Natal, and the Transvaal to escape

Dairy sign
Above: A vintage metal advertising sign promoting H. P. Hood & Sons's milk—and one of the dairy's workers.

Facing page: A completely contented cow
The friendly cow, all red and white,
I love with all my heart:
She gives me cream with all her might,
To eat with apple-tart. . . .
Robert Louis Stevenson (1850–1894) (Photo © Lynn Stone)

When a calf is born, its liver contains about a four-months' supply of iron and copper, useful in preventing anemia and in manufacturing red blood corpuscles. This is why calves' liver is so beneficial in treatment of human anemia.

Fold of Highland cattle
With their picturesque horns and long hair, Highlands may look a bit wild, but breeders claim they are not. Instead, they possess an indifference toward human beings that borders on disrespect because they have existed for centuries without a dependence upon people for their existence. (Photo © Lynn Stone)

Hereford bull

An 1884 engraving of an idealized Hereford bull, drawn in the typical "squared" styling of the day.

A cow's bowels may reach 170 feet (51 meters) in length.

British rule. The word *trek* is Afrikaans and means "draft."

North American Breeds

The wild American bison emigrated from Asia 25,000 years ago on the bridge formed by the Bering Strait and became the only cattle species native to America. Early European imports arrived by ship, having provided milk and meat for the lengthy voyage. Later, immigrant settlers brought cattle from their original homes. The Holstein dominates the North American dairy herd, exemplifying a major trend in North American cattle breeding: bigger is better, whereby bigger animals provide bigger yields. New genetic material is providing innovative cross-breeding possibilities.

One early crossbreed was the Cattalo, developed in 1894 at the Big Island Stock Farm near Bobcaygeon, Ontario. The Cattalo, a hybrid of domestic cattle and bison, was intended to take the fur and hump of the bison and place them on the back of the domestic ox. Continued experiments in Alberta determined that cattle-bison hybrids did have superior coats and winter foraging ability, but first-generation males proved sterile or of low fertility, and the project was abandoned in 1964.

Just as the Texas Longhorn developed from cattle brought up from Mexico, the Hawaiian Wild breed developed when cattle from Mexico and California were imported onto the island of Hawaii. At the beginning of the nineteenth century, these cattle were under royal protection and roamed freely in the sparsely populated hills of Mauna Kea. The animals multiplied rapidly, crossing with Durham, Angus, and Hereford, and the ban on hunting the Hawaiian Wild was lifted. Scores of the animals were killed for their hides, and by the 1970s, only one small herd of Hawaiian Wild cattle remained, preserved on a large estate.

The Canadian influence on North American cattle has been remarkable: Until the 1960s, the only major breeds of cattle imported from Europe to North America in any numbers were the standard dairy breeds and a few beef breeds, such as Angus and Hereford. A demand was developing for strains of beef cattle that would grow rapidly and produce more red meat with less fat. The quarantine against foot-and-mouth disease was primarily responsible for preventing any serious interest in any of the 200 different breeds of cattle available in Europe, although several breeds looked promising. In 1965, the Canadian government built a maximum quarantine station adequate to screen animals born in Europe for foot-and-mouth virus, and to introduce them into North America. The first new imports were French Charolais, followed by Simmental, Limousin, Maine-Anjou, Gelbvieh, Chianina, and about twenty other breeds. Most of the bulls had to remain in Canada for commercial reasons, so the only way to introduce them was through frozen semen and artificial insemination. Before long there were hundreds of thousands of cows in the United States bred to bulls of these new breeds, even though none of the bulls had stepped across the Canada–United States border. This activity generated a revolution in traditional livestock circles, and the exotic breeds brought fresh enthusiasm to an industry that had until then been ultraconservative.

It is possible to lead a cow upstairs but not downstairs, because a cow's knees cannot bend properly to walk back down.

Texas Longhorn in the Badlands
As with the Florida Cracker, the Texas Longhorn is considered one of the most adapted breeds in the southern United States, having existed for more than 500 years in North America under conditions that called for survival of the fittest. (Photo © Michael Francis)

> The age of a cow is always based on her age when she calves. This varies with different breeds. In other words, your record doesn't begin until you've had a calf, if you're a cow.

Randall Blue Lineback
This Randall Blue Lineback cow enjoying colorful autumn scenery in Connecticut is a variety of American Lineback, developed in the eastern United States and almost extinct today. (Photo © Lynn Stone)

Latin and South American Breeds

Like North America, the region comprising South America, Central America, and the Caribbean had no native cattle until Christopher Columbus brought cattle to the Island of Hispañola in 1493. After that, every Spanish ship that sailed for the Americas brought five or six head, and by 1525, there were a thousand head of cattle in the Caribbean colonies. Subsequent explorations spread Criollo cattle of Spanish or Portuguese origin to the mainland of Central and South America. These cattle were eventually crossed with European and/or zebu cattle, to influence many of the breeds currently favored there, including the San Martinero, Blanco Orejinegro, Costeño con Curnos, Indo-Brazilian, Nelore, and Romosinuano. In recent years, however, it has been the island of Jamaica that has seen major developments in cattle breeding, creating a successful new tropical dairy breed, the Jamaica Hope, which is 80 percent Jersey, 15 percent Sahiwal, and 5 percent Holstein.

Most of South America is dominated by beef cattle. Brazil has more head of cattle than any other South American country. Second is Argentina, which boasts 60 million cattle, or two and a half times as many cattle as people. These two countries account for three-quarters of South American beef. Brazil favors zebu and Criollo (known as Crioulo for their Portuguese origin) crosses. Aberdeen-Angus are especially popular in Argentina.

In Colombia, the Blanco Orejinegro (the name means "white black-eared") cattle are used for dairy and draft purposes on coffee plantations and as pack animals in the mountains. The San-

Sparring match
Making use of their extended horn spans, two Texas Longhorn bulls spar with each other. (Photo © Russell A. Graves)

When strange cows meet in the barnyard, there is a battle for dominance and hierarchy.

tander Hairless is found in Colombia, too, and although many have been inbred with American Brahman and Brown Swiss, one herd of Santander Hairless, with its unusually sparse, beige to light-red coat, has been preserved by the farmers' association of the district in the hope of producing good bulls to cross with zebu cattle.

Oceania Breeds
Similar to the American continents, New

Zealand and Australia had no indigenous cattle, and settlers were responsible for bringing them in during the nineteenth century. Initial Australian herds were a motley collection of shipboard animals that had supplied milk to travelers, with a few Indian zebu and some southern African cows. But improved British breeds appeared in the 1900s, with the Durham Shorthorn, Hereford, Aberdeen-Angus, Devon, and Red Poll becoming popular. In addition to basic British dairy breeds (Jersey, Holstein-Friesian, Ayrshire, Guernsey), Australia now also favors the Illawarra Shorthorn, found in the Illawarra region of southeastern New South Wales; this breed is kept for its high milk yield and moderate beef qualities. Most Australian dairy farms are family owned and operated, with almost all labor supplied by the farmer and his wife. The Hereford, Angus, and Shorthorn are still popular beef breeds, but the Murray Grey, Limousin, and Brahman are suited to the varied environment, as is the zebu-type Sahiwal, which was involved in the development of the Australian tropical dairy breeds, the Australian Milking Zebu and the Australian Friesian Sahiwal.

Although New Zealand has only 3.5 million people and 65 million sheep, the country finds room for a few million cattle. Angus and Hereford are popular beef breeds, along with Shorthorn, Murray Grey, Red Devon, Charolais, Simmental, South Devon, Limousin, and various crosses. Most New Zealand beef and veal is exported to North America.

New Zealand exports its dairy produce to twenty-eight countries. The country's more southerly latitudes encouraged specialization in dairying from the start, and there are 3.2 million dairy cattle on the islands, 90 percent of them on the North Island. Nearly all are Holstein, a quarter are Jersey, and the rest are mostly Holstein/Jersey crosses, Ayrshire, and Milking Shorthorn. A particular New Zealand breed, the Taurindicus, was developed at the famous Ruakura Agricultural Research Station. It combines the Sahiwal zebu's heat tolerance and disease/parasite resistance with the New Zealand Friesian's productivity. Until recently an old feral herd of Shorthorns

existed on subantarctic Enderby Island, in the Auckland Islands. The cattle had been more or less left alone since the 1890s.

Antarctica

The only cows ever known to visit Antarctica were four Guernseys: Deerfoot, Emmadine, Klondike and Iceberg, who accompanied Admiral Richard Byrd in his 1933 expedition to the South Pole. According to the Guernsey Cattle Club, "On Saturday, October 7, 1933, Admiral Richard E. Byrd asked for the loan of three Guernsey cows to take to the Antarctic with him in order that the men might have some fresh milk on the trip. Cows from Deerfoot Farms, South-boro, Massachusetts, Emmadine Farm, Hopewell Junction, New York and Klondike Farm, Ellan, North Carolina, were loaded on the supply ship *Jacob Ruppert*. In addition to sand and straw for bedding, a two-year supply of hay, beet pulp, grain and bran were loaded as well as a supply of milk bottle caps reading 'Byrd Antarctic Expedition, Golden Guernsey Milk Produced on Board the *Jacob Ruppert*.'"

The quiet Guernseys were good milkers and returned from Antarctica after 200,000 miles (320,000 km) of sea travel with a new bull calf, Iceberg, who was born on the way to the Antarctic Circle on December 19, 1933. Klondike, sadly, contracted frostbite during the trip and had to be destroyed.

Guernsey in Antarctica
In commemoration of the Guernsey's trek to Antarctica with Admiral Richard Byrd in 1933–1935, the American Guernsey Association struck this special medal.

In 1890, Thomas J. Hand described "The Bovine Species in General" in his book, *Milch Cows*. Of the udder, Hand wrote: "This organ is composed of the mammary glands, and the sac which contains them. The glands themselves should be elastic to pressure, and the skin thin, flexible, and covered with a fine, silky down, mounting to the upper limit of the sac, and extending down below towards the navel."

From Angus to Zebu: Cow Breeds of the World

God's jolly cafeteria
With four legs and a tail.
E. M. Root, *The Cow*

Texas Longhorn
Facing page: A longhorn cow on the Hope Ranch in Bonham, Texas. (Photo © Russell Graves)

Hereford on show
Right: A rancher leads a reluctant Hereford bull into the show ring. (Minnesota State Fair collection)

Angus

Originally from the shires of Aberdeen and Angus in northern Scotland, the Angus has been a popular beef breed for hundreds of years. The cattle of Aberdeen were affectionately referred to as

"hummlies," and those from Angus were called "doddies," but they were virtually the same. In 1873, four Angus bulls were imported to Kansas and shown at the Kansas City, Missouri, Livestock Exposition by George Grant, a Scottish cattleman who hoped to found a colony of wealthy British farmers in the United States. Over the next five years, 1,200 Angus cattle were imported from

Angus cow

The black hair and hide of Angus cattle are a trademark of the breed, and Angus are considered to be the ideal type of beef cattle. Originally from Scotland, Angus are naturally polled—born without horns. They are the most prominent of all the breeds known to have been bred exclusively for their beef from the very beginning. (Photo © Russell Graves)

Research has shown that scrotal circumference is related to increased sperm production in the bull and a younger age at puberty in his daughters.

Scotland, mainly to the American Midwest. In the first century of the American Aberdeen-Angus Breeders' Association, founded in Chicago in 1883, more than 10 million head were recorded. Today, the association records more cattle than any other beef breed association, making it the largest beef breed registry in the world. Angus are especially popular in Japan.

Ankole-Watusi

This breed can be traced back more than 6,000 years. They are also known as the "Cattle of Kings," and are traditionally considered sacred. Descended from the Egyptian or Hamitic Longhorn, the breed was well-established in the Nile Valley by 4,000 B.C., and their pictographs appear in Egyptian pyramids. Over the next twenty centuries, this Egyptian Longhorn breed followed its owners from the Nile to Ethiopia and into southern Africa where it bred with the zebu in 2,000 B.C. and became known as the Sanga, which spread to the Sudan, Uganda, Kenya, and other parts of eastern Africa.

Around the fourteenth century, the Watusi, or Tutsi, people arrived in Rwanda and Burundi, bringing massive-horned Ankole cattle with them, a strain of Sanga. These Watusi cattle so impressed the native Hutu tribe that the Watusi devised a way to exploit the situation. They loaned cows to the Hutu farmers who were allowed to look after them, milk them, and sometimes keep the bull calves; heifer calves were returned to the Watusi owners. For these "favors," the Hutu farmers cultivated the Watusi land and performed other services. In this manner, the Watusi people avoided work they considered menial and dominated the Hutu for centuries.

Today, the cattle found in Uganda, Rwanda, and Burundi are particularly notable, and possess different names. In Uganda, the Nkole tribe's variety of Sanga are known as the Ankole. In Rwanda and Burundi, the Tutsi tribe's variety are called the Watusi. The common Rwandan strain is called Inkuku. But the strain with giant horns, owned by the Tutsi kings and chiefs, is called the Inyambo; they are medium-sized cattle with incredibly large horns, and are regarded as sacred animals that are kept only by tribal chiefs and kings. Within some of these tribes, milking plays a role in tribal ritual: only virgins can milk cows, and cattle and milk are given a special place in ceremonial rites.

Watusi cattle are a sign of wealth within the tribe and are used as a form of barter and trade. They are also used as gifts to a bride's family at time of marriage. The animals are seldom slaughtered for meat except in ceremonies such as the coming of adulthood, but the cows are frequently milked and bled to make a clabbered, yogurtlike high-protein drink that is a staple in the diet.

Physically, Watusi cattle are striking. Nature developed characteristics to allow the survival of the breed in an area where, if a cow could not protect herself and her young from predators, she would be doomed to quick and violent extinction. The large-horned females are able to fend off groups of jackals or lions. Calves are born quickly and are able to outrun predators within a short amount of time. Cows produce a highly nutritious milk (butterfat tests out 7.3 percent) to nourish the young for speed and stamina. In addition to their incredible horns—the

largest and most dramatic of any breed—Watusi also have an extremely long, rope-like tail for swatting insects. According to the World Watusi Association, the cows and bulls are long legged, making them capable of running and jumping with tremendous agility. Cows have a small, tight udder that is not an easy target for predators or thorn bushes. Highly social, Watusi cows prefer to stay in a group for company and protection; "glum" is the term used for this social instinct of sticking together. At night, the cows tend to form a circle with adults ly-ing on the outside, horns out, to protect the calves located within. The calves will stay in groups by day, always in close proximity to at least one adult, and, when frightened, will instinctively run in front of the horns of a retreating mother or hide under her belly for safety.

The breed is especially resistant to drought, heat, and direct sunlight. Their digestive systems have the ability to uti lize poor-quality and limited quantities of food and water. In their native home-land, temperatures can soar to 120 de-grees Fahrenheit (49 degrees Celsius) and

Watusi steers

Because of their unusual appearance, Ankole-Watusi cattle were imported from Africa to European zoos and game parks in Germany, Sweden, and England during the late nine-teenth and early twentieth centuries. Ameri-can zoos and other tourist attractions im-ported them from European zoos in the 1920s and 1930s, and eventually Ankole-Watusi cattle became available for sale to private in-dividuals. (Photo © Cynthia Darling)

nights can plummet to 20°F (-6°C). The large horns act as radiators: blood circulating through the horn area is cooled and then returned to the main body with excess heat dispersed.

The Batawana, a related strain now nearly extinct, was described by Charles Darwin in 1868. The animal had horns of 104.3 inches (265 cm) in length, with a span of 161.02 inches (409 cm). In London's British Museum, the skull of a Batawana ox can be found, with horns 55.9 inches (142 cm) long and a span 100.78 inches (256 cm). Sometimes the colossal horns of this breed grew with enough weight, length, and leverage to deform the animal's skull. Few Batawana cattle remain today due to displacement by other breeds.

Ayrshire

The shire of Ayr in Scotland is the original home of the Ayrshire, a reddish-brown mahogany-and-white cow with jagged spots, imported into the United States by New England dairy farmers who needed cows to graze on their rough, rocky pastures and endure inhospitable winters. In 1929, "Tomboy" and "Alice," two Ayrshire cows, were walked from the Ayrshire Breeders' Association headquarters in Brandon, Vermont, to the National Dairy Show in St. Louis, Missouri, to prove their hardiness. For many years, the Ayrshire horns were a hallmark of the breed, curving gracefully out, up, and back. Unfortunately, the horns were not practical, and now almost all Ayrshires are dehorned as calves.

Beefalo

A full-blooded Beefalo is exactly three-eighths bison and five-eighths bovine,

with any of the beef breeds making up the latter. A cross between bison and bovine was not successful until the 1960s, and the hybrid provides "Beefalo Beef" that is lower in fat and cholesterol and high in protein. The addition of bison genetics to beef cattle contributes hybrid vigor due to generations of bison survival on the North American plains where herds grew to number between sixty million and a hundred million.

Black Baldy

Black Baldy is not an official breed, but is the name of the white-faced black cattle seen on many farms and ranches. The cross between Polled Hereford and Angus is one of the most popular feedlot animals.

Blonde d'Aquitaine

The Blonde d'Aquitaine is a wheat-colored French breed that can be traced back to cattle of the sixth century when blonde cattle were used to pull carts of weapons and other goods plundered by eastern conquerors across Germany and Gaul (France) into Spain and Portugal. They were considered a triple-purpose breed then, used for milk and meat as well as oxen. Three strains of cattle make up this breed: the Garonnais, Quercy, and Blonde des Pyrenees. The Garonnais oxen worked in ports and vineyards and pulled barges before they were replaced by horses and the steam engine.

Brahman

India has at least thirty well-defined breeds of cattle, and three principal strains were used in the development of the American Brahman breed: the Guzerat, a highly revered beast of burden

In Skinner's *Treatise on Milch Cows* (1846), the author lists, in order of personal preference, the names of the eight classes of cattle to be assigned by the reader to "any Cow examined by him to her appropriate place in the classification, and consequently form an accurate judgment in regard to the maximum quantity of milk which she can yield daily." The classifications are: "The Flanders Cow, The Selvage Cow, The Curveline Cow, The Bicorn Cow, The Demijohn Cow, The Square Scutcheon Cow, The Limousine Cow, and the Horizontal Cut Cow."

Ayrshire cow
Facing page: The Ayrshire, the only breed of the six major dairy breeds in the world today to be developed on the main isle of Great Britain, was native to the highlands of County Ayr, Scotland, where thrifty Scottish farmers wanted a dairy cow with a healthy constitution to withstand the rugged highland weather and an ability to make an economic return on scanty rations. The Ayrshire was known by several names during its development, including Cunningham and Dunlop. Cheese made in Ayrshire, Scotland, was known as Dunlop cheese. (Photo © Lynn Stone)

Brahma cow

Brahman cattle are intelligent, inquisitive, and shy. Despite their somewhat fearsome appearance, they like affection and can become docile. In Brazil and elsewhere in Latin America, all *Bos indicus* cattle, such as the Brahman and other breeds with large humps, curved horns, and pendulous ears, came to be called zebu. (Photo © Russell Graves)

in India, a symbol to the Hindus of the idyllic pastoral life and traced back to 3,000 B.C. by carvings found in archaeological excavations in Pakistan; the Nelore or "the poor man's cow," generally found in small village herds and the breed found in the greatest numbers in India; and the Gir, raised in many parts of India, known for its prominent forehead, pendulous ears, smooth conformation, and docile temperament. Because all cattle are considered sacred in India by those of the Hindu faith, they are not

permitted to be slaughtered or sold and have developed a natural resistance to inadequate food, insects, parasites, and diseases of the tropical country.

The first Indian cattle were reportedly imported to South Carolina in 1849 by Dr. James Bolton Davis, who had served as agricultural advisor to the Sultan of Turkey. In 1854, cotton farmer Richard Barrow of St. Francisville, Louisiana, was presented by Great Britain with two Indian bulls in gratitude for teaching cotton and sugar cane production to British officials who were establishing these crops in the deltas of India.

Like all *Bos indicus* cattle, the Brahman have a large hump over the top of the shoulder and neck, curved horns, and large, pendulous ears. Their heat tolerance is remarkable: European cattle begin to suffer as temperatures rise above 75°F (24°C), showing an increase in body temperature and a decline in appetite and milk production, but Brahman cattle show little effect from temperatures up to and beyond 105°F (40°C). The great amount of excess skin in the throat latch and dewlap aids the Brahman's ability to withstand warm weather by increasing the body surface area exposed to cooling. In cold weather, the skin contracts, increasing the thickness of the hide and the density of the hair, which helps to retain body heat. When winters are severe, Brahmans grow a protective covering of long, coarse hair over a downy, fur-like undercoat. Another special quality of this breed is the presence of more highly developed sweat glands than those of European cattle. And they produce an oily secretion from the sebaceous glands that has a distinctive odor and helps to repel insects.

Braunvieh

Referred to in Canada as Beef Brown Swiss, *Braunvieh* is a German word meaning "Brown Cow." These cattle may date back to the Bronze Age; some think it is the oldest pure breed on earth. An account from the nineteenth century describes the Swiss scenery where Braunvieh grazed, 3,000–8,500 feet (900–2,550 meters) above sea level: "There are throughout the whole mountain region of Switzerland high valleys and steep pastures to which the cattle are driven in May or June and graze until the end of the brief summer. Even there, the same zealous and intelligent care is taken to protect animals from every contingency of weather. The chalets on the lofty meadows, which look so picturesque from the valleys below, are, for the most part, cowhouses built of squared logs or planks carefully chinked with clay or moss and constructed like the barns for winter, in the most careful and substantial manner. Nine layers or thicknesses of shaved pine shingles are used in the roofs of these chalets, so carefully are they constructed to exclude the damp and cold. There is often a fireplace between the stalls at the end opposite the door, and there the mountain herdsman lives and sleeps with his cows from spring until autumn. If the morning is fair and the sun warm he turns them out to graze upon the short, sweet mountain grass, and busies himself with mowing and bringing in a supply that will serve to sustain his herd during night or stormy weather; but at the first approach of cold wind or rain his 'jodel' is heard and the cows hasten to their accustomed shelter. Naturally, purely blooded cattle treated in this way, curried and brushed daily like well-kept horses, trained to be led and handled, always cared for, have become in the course

Brangus bull
The Brangus, a cross between Brahman and Angus, is considered by many beef cattle producers to be the most trouble-free cow in the industry. More than half of the twenty-five largest beef cattle producers in the United States run Brangus cattle, and the breed adapts well to any climate. Registered Brangus must be solid black, polled, and be three-eighths Brahman and five-eighths Angus.

British White cow and calf
There is much confusion in North America between the White Park breed of cattle and the British White. The White Park, used mostly for beef, is smaller than the British White, and occasionally horned. The British White, on the other hand, is genetically polled, docile, and was a dual-purpose beef and milk breed until 1950. (Photo © Morris Halliburton)

of generations perfectly domesticated."

Today roughly 40 percent of the cattle in Switzerland are Braunvieh. Between 1869 and 1880, approximately 130 head of Braunvieh were imported into the United States, where they became the basis for development of the American Brown Swiss dairy breed. Now Brown Swiss may be found in Canada, Mexico, and other Latin countries. Canada imported its first Braunvieh, a bull, in 1968.

British White

The British White is a primitive breed that dates back to the eighth or ninth century in Scandinavia and was brought into Britain by Vikings. They are sometimes confused with White Park cattle, but they are not the same: Ancient White Park have lyre-shaped horns, are semi-wild, and can be dangerous. The British White, however, is polled and docile, and served as a beef and milk breed until 1950 when it began to be bred specifically for beef production. During World War II, Winston Churchill issued an order calling for all crops to be burned and cattle to be slaughtered if the Germans invaded England. To ensure the preservation of British White seed stock, breeders shipped five cows and one bull to the United States. After the war, the cattle ended up in Illinois.

American White Park is a large white breed with black or red ears, nose, and eyes, and is noted for its strong maternal instinct and ease of calving. It is used for beef in the United States, but it is descended from the British White and should not be confused with the ancient British White Park, a separate and unrelated breed.

In 1941, on the brink of the German

Heifers that conceive earlier are likely to have a longer and more productive life in the herd.

Brown Swiss cow in the Swiss Alps
The Brown Swiss is a large, docile breed from the Swiss Alps, whose distinctive strength and ruggedness is due to its arduous origins. In spring, the cattle would be sent into the mountains with caretakers and cheesemakers, where they would graze at altitudes of 3,000 to 8,500 feet (900–2,550 meters) for 90 to 115 days, existing on native vegetation with no supplemental feed even for lactating cows. (Photo © Lynn Stone)

Brown Swiss cows
Above: These Brown Swiss cows on Vermont's Shelburne Farms produce milk for some of the finest cheddar cheese (for sale at the farm and by mail order) in New England. The site of thirty smaller farms, the original acreage was purchased in the late nineteenth century by William Seward Webb and his wife, Lila Vanderbilt Webb, who wished to make Shelburne Farms a model for the latest in agricultural techniques and technology; the land has remained in the family ever since. (Photo © Lynn Stone)

Brown Swiss cow
Right: Portrait of a Brown Swiss herd. (Brown Swiss Cattle Breeders' Association)

invasion of England, five British White cows and one bull were shipped to a Pennsylvania prison farm where they were held until 1949. These original British White cattle, plus several other full-blood British Whites imported from England, form the foundation of today's British White herds in North America. One of the most famous American White Park bulls, "Old Ugly," was an original "penitentiary bull," according to the breed association. His progeny can still be found in many American White Park herds throughout the United States.

Brown Swiss

Also known as Brown Shwyzer, the Brown Swiss is one of the oldest dairy breeds in the world. It is descended from the Braunvieh, but may go back to Oriental origins, although cattle bones found among ruins of Swiss Lake Dwellers are similar to the bones of the current Brown Swiss. The large, docile breed is valued for its strength and ruggedness. When judging this cow in competition during the mid-1800s, consideration had to be given to whether the animal had been stabled or "alped," because differences in activity, environment, quantity, and quality of food supply had marked effects on the size and condition of the animal.

The Herens, another breed native to the Swiss Alps, was originally a sporting breed in which the herd leaders were specially trained for the cowfight in which animals pushed against each other, head to head, until the loser backed away.

Camargue

Somewhat similar in appearance to the Kerry of Ireland, the Camargue are found in the isolated Rhône delta of France, called the Camargue. There they live in a semiwild state and are herded by riders similar to American cowboys. The cattle are raised for beef, but the bulls are selected for a form of bloodless bullfighting. A team of twelve men use small tridents to attempt to remove a rosette of ribbons attached to the horns. The bull wins if he keeps the rosette after fifteen minutes. The main danger to the men is from the bull's horns, but the bull always leaves the arena unharmed.

In the 1930s when Lutz Heck was looking for breeding stock to reproduce the aurochs, he purchased several of the Camargue breed. "The noble, fiery cattle of the Camargue are bred simply and purely in order to bring honour and fame to their owner in the bull-fights that have been carried on from ancient times in the south of France," he wrote. "These fights are totally different from the Spanish ones; the animal is not killed, but a dangerous game is played, in which men's lives may be at stake. A bright little woollen tassel is fastened to each horn, a cockade is fixed in the middle of the animal's forehead, and these have to be captured. It is a battle in the arena between a raging, roaring bull and twenty agile men, who try to snatch the trophies from its forehead. . . . Almost every Sunday in spring this bull-fight takes place in every town and even

Canadienne cow

The Canadienne is the result of a blend of livestock imported from Normandy and Brittany, but today a Canadienne breed society has been formed to save the cow from extinction. (Photo © Alan Ross, Three Creek Farm)

Corriente

Above: The Corriente are most familiar to fans of rodeo, where the cattle are used as roping steers and in bull dogging, cattle cutting, and other rodeo events like wild-cow milking and team branding. (Photo © Russell Graves)

Bullriding

Below: The tough rodeo sport of bullriding is not as simple as hanging on for a brief time while the bull bucks and twists his way out of the chute. Special equipment is required, including bullropes, bells, spurs, and pads. Sometimes getting off the mad bull holds even more risk for the cowboy than riding it. (Photo © Jerry Irwin)

the smallest villages in Provence. On the Saturday herdsmen on horseback drive the strongest and best-formed cattle from the meadows to an enclosure by the arena. Bulls, oxen and cows are used for the fights. The selection of the cattle from the herd is a dangerous undertaking, for the infuriated animals try again and again to break away. When at last the herdsmen have rounded them up on a main road, they drive the animals at a gallop, as fast as their horses can go, to make it impossible for them to turn back. The little crowd of riders and furious cattle come like a cloud of dust to the place of the fight, where the population greet them enthusiastically on their arrival. The cattle are kept in secure custody until the next day: they refuse fodder and water, because, living as wild animals, they know only the meadow and are not used to eating and drinking from receptacles."

Canadienne

This breed—also known as the Canadian, Black Canadian, or French Canadian—is the result of a blend of livestock imported into Canada from Normandy and Brittany during the sixteenth and seventeenth centuries. In the early 1540s, Jacques Cartier brought cattle of Norman and Breton stock to New France, followed by Samuel de Champlain's imports in 1608–1610. Although it adapted to the harsh climate of Quebec, the breed was discouraged by the Council of Agriculture until by 1880 "there was hardly a French Canadian in the Province that thought enough of his cow to give her more attention than he would a dog," according to the Canadian Rare Breeds Conservancy. A breed society was formed to save the Canadienne from extinction. The new breed, "La Canadienne," remains the only dairy breed today to have been developed on the North American continent.

Charolais

These cattle are large, white with pigmented skin, horned, good milkers, and have a short hair coat in summer that thickens and lengthens in cold weather. They originated as a triple-purpose breed (draft, milk, and meat) in west-central to southeastern France in the old provinces of Charolles and Nievre where they were selected and bred for their color. French growers also stressed size and muscling, with little attention to refinement.

Charolais came into the United States from a herd in Mexico where they were imported soon after World War I by a Mexican industrialist who had served as a volunteer in the French army.

Chianina

The world record for cattle size was set in 1955 by the Chianina bull, Conetto, who weighed 3,836 pounds (1,740 kg). The Chianina are the largest breed of cattle in the world: The average Chianina cow weighs 1,874 pounds (850 kg) with a height of 63 inches (160 cm) at the withers. Bulls average 2,678.5 pounds (1,215 kg) and measure 67.3 inches (171 cm) at the withers, but often grow much larger.

Originally from the Chiana valley of Tuscany, porcelain-white varieties of Chianina can be found throughout Italy and have been exported for cross-breeding all around the globe. This is an old breed, praised by Georgic poets Columella and Virgil, and used as models for Roman sculptures. Until recently, Chianina were primarily used as draft animals, but selection now emphasizes beef production. U.S. servicemen stationed in Italy during World War II discovered the Chianina, and the first semen was introduced to this country in 1971.

Corriente

The Corriente were the first cattle brought to the New World by the Spanish, as early as 1493, and they had to be a hardy breed to endure the ocean crossing. After their arrival in Florida and the West Indies, Corriente were also taken to Central and South America. Pure strains of this breed exist only in small numbers today, although the original Corriente were used for milk, meat, and draft purposes across the southern United States and up the coast of California. Corriente breeders today usually sell the year's production to rodeo contractors, but other ranchers may lease their roping steers and heifers to stock contractors or roping clubs on a monthly basis.

Devon

The Devon is sometimes referred to as "North Devon" to distinguish it from the South Devon, and is also given the nickname "Red Rubies" for the preferred bright ruby-red color. Some think the Devon's origin may be prehistoric—that the Devon descended directly from the aboriginal *Bos longifrons* and contributed

to the Hereford and other British breeds. Native to Devon, Somerset, and Dorset, this breed caught the eye of the Romans who occupied the area in 55 B.C. Later, when an invasion by Napoleon was anticipated in Devon, a notice was issued in a local church directing all stock to be slaughtered if the community was taken unawares; otherwise the cattle were to be driven into Somerset or Dartmoor.

A consignment of Devon cattle arrived at the Plymouth Colony in North America in 1623. Devon oxen were highly prized in the American Colonies for their strength, intelligence, endurance, and fast pace. Even today, Devons are sought for use as oxen.

Dexter

Dexter are tiny black cattle, one of the smallest breeds in the world. Some believe them to be a branch of the Kerry breed. Dexters were first reported in Ireland in 1776. There they flourished and roamed almost wild around the shelterless mountain districts in the late 1800s, where they were bred by farmers with only small pieces of land. Despite their size, they are considered fine dairy animals and are considered the perfect, old-fashioned "family cow." The ideal Dexter cow measures between 35 to 42 inches (87.5–105 cm) at the shoulder and weighs less than 750 pounds (337.5 kg), but a milking cow can produce more milk for its

Chianina cow
Above: The largest cattle in the world, the Chianina is often referred to as a "terminal" breed by ranchers, meaning that the primary use is as the sire to animals that will be marketed. The herds in which they are used are frequently crossbred, and Chianina bulls provide an outstanding growth rate in the offspring of the crossbred females. (Photo © Russell Graves)

Charolais
Below: It has been said that no other breed has impacted the North American beef industry as significantly as the introduction of the Charolais, which were incorporated when American breeders were seeking larger-framed, heavier cattle than traditional British breeds. (Photo © Russell Graves)

Devon cow
In England, the Devon are known as "The Beef Breed Supreme at Grass," and they have grown in popularity in southern Brazil, Australia, and New Zealand. The Milking Devon is descended from this triple-purpose stock; it has the same bright ruby-red color with an elegant form and curving horns. (Photo © Lynn Stone)

weight than any other breed. The daily yield averages 1.5 to 2.5 gallons (5.7–9.5 liters), with a butterfat content of 4 to 5 percent. Yields of cream up to one quart per one gallon (0.95 liters per 3.8 liters) are possible.

Because they do well on marginal or scrub land, Dexters are popular in Australia and South Africa. Although there are more than 350 breeders of Dexters in Canada and the United States, they are a rare breed in North America, and semen is stored by the American Minor Breeds Conservancy (AMBC).

Dutch Belted

Lakenvelder means "sheeted," and that's what this breed is sometimes called because the cattle look like they have been wrapped with white sheets or belts around the middle. Due to their distinctive appearance, the Lakenvelders were sought by kings and noblemen, cultured artists and ordinary farmers. *Gurtenvieh*, or "canvassed," cattle in Switzerland and Austria were moved from their mountain

farms by Dutch nobility soon after the feudal period. Other belted animals became popular as well, including rabbits, chickens, goats, and pigs.

In 1840, P. T. Barnum imported Dutch Belted cattle to the United States for exhibition in his great circus, where they were featured for several years. Later the Barnum cattle were placed on a farm, and this seems to have been the beginning of the Dutch Belted breed in the United States. From 1915 to 1940, the Lakenvelder flourished, but they are now listed as critically rare by the American Livestock Breeds Conservancy. This is crucial, since the breed in the United States is the only source of pure belted genetics in the world: The Lakenvelders in the Netherlands suffered from crossbreeding between 1950 and 1976, and Dutch breeders must turn to American Dutch Belted breeders for semen from pure bulls.

The milk contains tiny fat globules, almost as if it were already homogenized. This makes Dutch Belted milk highly digestible, and it also has a high butterfat content.

Florida Cracker

The name *Corriente* sometimes becomes "Criollo" in Central and South America, and in Florida the few remaining small,

Dexter bull and cow
Dexters are one of the smallest breeds in physical size. They may be found in three colors: red, black, or dun, and may be found in two types: the longleg and the shortleg. Both types produce similar amounts of meat or milk. (Photo © Sara Rath)

native cattle—cousins of the Mexican Corriente—are called Scrub Cattle, Cracker Cattle, Piney Woods, or Florida Native. The colony of St. Augustine was stocked with Cuban cattle when it was established in 1565; these were Criollo ancestors of the Florida Cracker that became a hardy breed through hundreds of years of existence as a feral animal, existing on thick and heavily wooded lowland areas where the breed evolved to withstand heat, insects, and humidity. It is a small animal with a narrow build and large barrel, due to the unusually great amount of roughage in its diet. The name *Cracker* is taken from the cracking sound of the herdsman's bullwhip.

By 1970, there were only a few isolated herds of purebred Florida Scrub, and in 1971, a bull and several cows were presented to the state of Florida in an attempt to save the breed from extinction. At the present time, herds are maintained at Payne's Prairie State Park near Gainesville; Lake Kissimmee State Park near Lake Wales; and Withlacoochee State Forest near Brooksville. Similar cattle in Louisiana are known as Louisiana Scrub. See Texas Longhorn for the Lone Star State's equivalent of this historic breed.

Fulani

South of the Sahara Desert a belt of savanna spreads from Lake Chad to Senegal, providing a relatively dry country and Africa's main cattle region. This is home to the Fulani breed, owned by the nomadic Cattle Fulani herdsmen who regard their cattle as capital; the animals are a form of currency valued in bride-wealth, for example.

The cows are milked but rarely slaughtered, although the tribes will sell the cattle for slaughter by others, and the herds are a major source of meat for the densely populated southern coastal regions of West Africa. During periods of major drought, tribes survive by drinking the cattle's milk and blood. Some of the Fulani have dramatic, lyre-shaped horns that sweep upward, and a herd can resemble a dense forest of horns.

Galloway

In 1926, the famous Montgomery Ward mail-order catalog featured Galloway coats: "Whether you're 20 and want to be in correct style or 40 and want complete warmth from head to foot, you'll like the quality and workmanship of this natural black Galloway fur coat and you'll like the savings it brings you for $45."

The Galloway is an ancient Scottish breed, native to the shires of Dumfries, Lanark, Renfew, Ayr, Kirkudbright, and Wigtown in the Scottish Lowlands, where the cattle of the region went unnamed for centuries, referred to only as "the black cattle of Galloway." In the eighteenth century, Scottish farmers began to breed selectively for the polled factor (it occurred by spontaneous mutation once in every 50,000 births, even if it wasn't deliberately introduced) in order to make the shaggy black cattle of Galloway easier to manage on the long droves to London markets.

Galloway is derived from *Gallovid*, which in old Scot signifies "a Gaul." Noted by historians for their thick, wooly double hair coat and hornless condition, Galloway emerged as the beef breed of choice in the fifteenth and sixteenth centuries, and continued to dominate the England and Scotland beef trade for

Florida Cracker cow
A rare breed, the Florida Cracker, also known as Piney Woods or Florida Native, are descended from cattle brought to St. Augustine from Cuba in 1565. (Photo © Dr. Tim Olson)

The heaviest recorded live birth weight for a calf is 225 pounds: This was a British Friesian cow at Rockhouse Farm in Great Britain in 1961.

Cows, if left alone, can be expected to live to be about eighteen years of age. There are exceptions, however—old-timers who make it to twenty-five or thirty. You cannot tell the age of a cow just by looking at it. There used to be a rule that said to count the rings on the horns and add two, for a cow; for a bull, count the rings on the horns and add five. But the rule of thumb wasn't always accurate due to unscrupulous cattle dealers who would file a few rings off the old horns to erase a couple of years.

Dutch Belted cattle

A herd of these cattle in a pasture can cause quite a sensation to onlookers expecting traditional black-and-white Holsteins, and seeing instead the Dutch Belted cattle that look like Holsteins with a broad white stripe. The Lakenvelder, or "sheeted" cattle, were bred by Dutch noblemen because they wanted their cows to look different from those of the common farmers. Oddly, the Lakenvelder and other belted cattle have black tongues. (Photo © Bruce Fritz)

Galloway calves
Introduced to Scotland by ninth-century Vikings, Galloways are the oldest known British breed of record. These Galloway calves exhibit typical color variations and the traditional furry Galloway coat. (Photo © Susan Waples)

Belted Galloway herd
The "belt" is a dominant genetic trait, and the Belted Galloway, or "Beltie," will exist in almost all Galloway calves sired by a Belted bull. (Photo © Keith Baum)

hundreds of years. Most Galloways are black, but they may also be red, dun, or white with black ears, eyes, nose, hooves, and teats, and there are also Belted Galloways, introduced in the seventeenth or eighteenth century with the infusion of Dutch Belted blood. The Belted Galloways are sometimes known as "Belties."

The Galloway is said to be fierce in protecting its calf from predators. In fact, the calf in distress doesn't even have to be her own. Breeders in Montana, North Dakota, and Iowa report the ability of Galloway cows to repel wolves, coyotes, and coyote-dogs, and some farmers even use Galloways as guardian animals for flocks of sheep. In Kenya, Galloways protect their calves from hyenas. One rancher says, "We need to proclaim the superiority of the Galloway cow—intelligent, courageous, and fully committed to protecting her baby."

Ganado Bravo

Bred in Spain for their aggressive nature, strength, and vigor, the Ganado Bravo (also known as Toro de Lidia, Toro Lidiado, and Guro de Lide) fighting bulls have long curved necks and elegant stature. Color is not important. The bull holds his head high and is able to achieve remarkable speed and agility due to long, slender legs. Ganado Bravo are also found in Portugal and South and Central America where bullfights are organized.

Portugal is also home to the Mértola breed, now being developed as beef animals. The Mertola oxen, known for their docility, are frequently used to herd fighting bulls in the Ribatejo region of Portugal and to lead the bull from the arena after the bullfight (in Portugal the bull is not killed in public). This herding and

Bullfight advertisement
Postcard for a bullfight at La Paloma bullring in Puerto Vallarta, Mexico.

guiding capability is shared by the Spanish Pied, or Berrenda, breed, and breeders of fighting cattle often use Spanish Pied oxen as guide animals for their high-spirited herds.

Mammal zoologist Lutz Heck wrote that the Spanish fighting bull "has been bred from old almost without change. The bulls are smaller than those in Germany; what matters in the bull-fight is not the animal's size but its fire, agility, and courage. The bulls are tested in the meadows: men on horseback attack them with short blunt lances, and they are valued according to their reaction; the 'cowards' revealed by this test are relentlessly eliminated.

"Thus the Spanish fighting-bull is one of the few animals deliberately bred for definite 'spiritual' qualities. It must

Gelbvieh bull
Like most European breeds, the Gelbvieh was originally a triple-purpose breed. Also known as *Einfarbig gelbes Hohenvich*, or German Yellow, the Gelbvieh is from Bavaria, in southern Germany, and is one of the European breeds introduced to the United States through artificial insemination. Since World War II, Germany has used a stringent selection program to repopulate its cattle herds. Only 3 percent of the registered cows are used to produce potential bulls, and bulls are given a rigorous battery of performance and progeny tests. (Photo © American Gelbvieh Association)

Guernsey cow painting
Above: Portrait of a Guernsey cow. (American Guernsey Association)

Guernsey cows in the dandelions
Right: The Guernsey is known for producing milk with high butterfat and high protein content, as well as high betacarotene concentration—thus "Golden Guernsey" milk. The first Guernsey in the United States came ashore in 1830 or 1831, brought by a Boston sea captain who stopped at the Island of Guernsey and picked up two young cows and a bull to give to his brother who owned a farm on Cow Island in Lake Winnepesaukee, New Hampshire. One of the cows died soon afterward, but the remaining cow and bull became the foundation of the first herd. (Photo © Lynn Stone)

Like the hog callers in the American Midwest, country folk in England had special cries to summon their cows. For cows they'd yell, "Coop!" "Cush, cush!" "Hoaf!" "Hobe!" "Mull!" "Proo!" or "Proochy! Prut!" To call calves, they shout, "Moodie!" "Mog, mog mog!" "Puihoi!" or "Sook, sook!"

not only have speed in running and agility in turning, but must have the right mentality for the bull-ring, ferocity in at once attacking every opponent that shows himself, and resolution in continuing the fight in spite of wounds. It must be eager to fight to the death."

Guernsey

The Island of Guernsey consists of only twenty-four square miles (62 sq-km). The island is smaller, colder, gets more rain, and is less fertile than the Isle of Jersey, twenty-two miles south (35 km), but these two Channel Islands share a distinction in being the home islands of two fine dairy breeds.

In his book, *Breeds of Cattle* (1987), renowned cattle judge Herman Purdy describes the Guernsey's background: "In the dark ages of religious persecution, the Channel Islands were a place of refuge for those banished from the continent. When he was exiled from France, Victor Hugo spent much time at his home on Guernsey and wrote some famous works there.

"In A.D. 960, one of the Normandy rulers was informed that his island of Guernsey had become a haven to pirates who were stirring up trouble with the native inhabitants. He sent a colony of monks from St. Michael in Brittany to establish an abbey there and teach the islanders how to farm better and how to defend themselves. The monks, once on Guernsey, sent back to Brittany for the 'Froment de Leon' breed of cow, a small brown and white producer of rich milk. In 1060 other monks from Cherbourg, Normandy, brought the larger brindle cattle from the Province of Isigny over to Guernsey. Crosses between these two

Cattle can perceive higher and fainter noises than humans can, and they can smell scents that are up to six miles away (if the wind is right).

Hereford cows and calf
Two and a half centuries ago, the Hereford breed was established to provide beef for the expanding food market created by Britain's Industrial Revolution. The cattle boasted a high yield of beef and efficiency of production, and these characteristics remain today as outstanding traits of the breed. (Photo © Lynn Stone)

breeds resulted in the Guernsey, although the Guernsey probably has more blood of the Normandy cattle and the Jersey breed more of the Brittany. Also, infusion of the blood of Danish cattle may have become part of the Guernsey background when Danes occupied the Channel Islands.

"The Guernsey has a mellow color, pleasing to the eye—a shade of fawn with white markings of clearly defined borders. The switch of the tail is white and flowing. Often a spot or patch of white shows high on the forehead."

Hereford

Thrifty and enterprising Benjamin Tomkins of Herefordshire, England, is considered the father of the familiar red-bodied, white-faced Hereford breed. In 1742, Tomkins used cows Pidgeon and Mottle, inherited from his father's estate, and bred them to a bull calf from the cow, Silver. He wished to establish beef cattle that were hardy, had early maturity, and had a natural aptitude to grow and gain from grass and grain—traits that are of primary importance in the Hereford breed today.

Herefords were imported into the United States in 1817 by statesman Henry Clay of Kentucky, but the first real breeding herd arrived in Albany, New York, in 1840; New York State Fair records from 1844 indicate eleven Herefords exhibited that summer, with high praise. The Hereford breed expanded rapidly after the Civil War with the advance of the Industrial Revolution and westward expansion. Western ranching was developing from free land and local longhorned cattle that had been allowed to drift northward into what became southwestern cattle country. The long-horns were tough, with an inbred ability to survive, and demand for Hereford bulls, who became known as "the great improver" of western cattle, was enthusiastic. Only 200 head of Herefords had been imported up to 1880, but more than 3,500 head came over from England during the years 1880 to 1889. The greatest Hereford bull, Anxiety 4, was imported during that time: He was given the name "Father of American Herefords," and "the bull that gave Herefords hindquarters." Anxiety 4 is the common ancestor of nearly all Hereford cattle in this country today.

The Polled Hereford is the Hereford minus the horns, developed by Midwestern Hereford breeders. Unlike many other cattle, the Polled Hereford began in the United States and was exported to England in the 1950s.

The Braford is a combination of three-fourths Brahman and five-eighths Hereford. This hardy and popular breed was developed in 1947 by Alto Adams, Jr. on his ranch in St. Lucie County, Florida, to adapt to the specific environment of south Florida.

Highland

This picturesque and shaggy deep red breed with long eyelashes and tousled forelocks has been a part of the raw landscape of the Scottish Highlands as far back as the twelfth century. Since they ran wild in the Scottish Highlands, only those strains that could adapt to the rigorous weather were encouraged to survive, and no other breed has retained greater uniformity. Thus, the breed became hardy, thrifty, disease resistant, and developed good mothering ability. A

The two most hardy breeds of cattle in the world today are the yak and the Scottish Highland. Both breeds are heavy milkers.

How to Say Cowpie in Eight Languages

Cowpie, meadow muffin, cow flop, cow chip—here's a handy reference to say "cow droppings" in eight different languages:

Danish: *Kokasser*
Dutch: *Koeievlaaien*
French: *Bouse de Vache*
German: *Kuhfladen*
Gujurati: *Chhaan*
Japanese: *Ushi no foon*
Norwegian: *Kuruke*
Swedish: *Dynga* or *koblaffa*

Scottish Highland cow
Why is this cow smiling? The Scottish Highland is one of the two most hardy breeds of cattle in the world today, along with the yak. (Photo © Lynn Stone)

Highland cow will nurse her calf for eleven months or more, if permitted. Originally there were two classes of Highland cattle: the smaller, black Kyloe, from the islands off the west coast of Scotland; and the larger, redder animal from the remote Highlands. Today both are regarded as one breed. Several strains have superior milking ability and were selected to provide the home milk supply for Scottish crofters, or small tenant farmers. Highland milk has a high butterfat content, averaging 7 percent, but sometimes more than 10 percent.

It has been said that the Highland will eat what other cattle pass by, and get fat on it. Extremely intelligent, they do not stress easily, are disease resistant, and even tempered. Like bison, Highland cattle face into the snow and wind during a storm; the long foretop protects the face, and the wind blows the long coat flat rather than ruffling it up. They have a double coat of hair—a downy undercoat and a long outercoat which may reach thirteen inches (32.5 cm) and is well oiled to shed rain and snow. They do not begin to lose body heat until temperatures reach -18°F (-10°C), which means they need little or no grain to keep warm. In Canada, many Highland folds, or herds, are situated in areas where other cattle would not be able to survive and reproduce in the severe climate. The breed is now found throughout North America, Europe, Australia, and South America.

Breeders in Scotland call their herds of Highland cattle "folds," instead of herds. Her Majesty the Queen of England maintains a fold of Highland cattle at Balmoral Castle. On the big cattle estates in Scotland it is common practice to breed Highland females with a beef Shorthorn bull, then breed the female progeny to a Hereford or Angus bull. A new fixed breed, the Luing, is gaining in

A Holstein calf named *Christmas* holds the record for the lowest live birth weight at only nine pounds. She was born December 25, 1993 on the farm of Mark and Wendy Theuinger in Hutchinson, Minnesota.

Milking school

A group of students at the University of Minnesota learn the intricacies of milking a Holstein in the 1940s. (Photo © Minneapolis Public Library, Minneapolis Collection)

popularity with cattlemen and butchers throughout Britain; the Luing is three-eighths Highland and five-eighths Shorthorn.

Holstein

The Holstein is the premier dairy cow of the world. It is the most numerous and the most popular dairy breed. The original stock were black animals and white animals belonging to migrant European tribes, the Batavians and Friesians, who settled in the Rhine Delta about 2,000 years ago. The black-and-white spotted breed with which we are so familiar originated in the late 1700s in the Netherlands where much of the land, reclaimed from the sea with an elaborate system of dikes, is costly and must be used efficiently. In turn, efficiency and productivity became benchmarks in the development of this breed. After being turned out to pasture in early May, milk cows were kept in pastures divided by drainage ditches rather than fences and were often protected from the elements in early and late pasturing seasons with rugs and blankets. Milkers often went into the field to do their milking there. In winter, the cattle were housed in stables that often shared a roof with the farmhouse. Almost no animal older than six or seven years was kept unless she was an exceptional milker. By 1865, these were known as "Holland" cattle, the most famous of which was the strain called Friesian.

In 1852, Massachusetts breeder Winthrop Chenery purchased a Holland cow from a Dutch sailing master who landed in Boston with his cargo. The cow had produced fresh milk for the crew during the voyage, and Chenery was so pleased with her that he made more importations of the breed, and others fol-lowed. The name "Holstein" was an accidental label, for Holstein, Germany, had no significant connection with Dutch cattle brought to the United States.

The Holstein breed is most prominent in Wisconsin, New York, Pennsylvania, Minnesota, and California, but it is present throughout North America and, indeed, throughout the world. Holsteins may be red and white, as well as black and white. Ninety percent of all milk consumed in the United States comes from Holsteins. Early and widespread use of artificial insemination occurred with this breed, but it is the only breed that cannot be improved upon with regard to milk production when bred to another, making Holsteins unique in the world of cattle breeding.

Jamaica Hope

Named after Hope Farm, the Jamaican government farm where the breed was originally developed, the Jamaica Hope is a combination of Jersey (80 percent), Sahiwal (15 percent), and Holstein (5 percent), leading the Caribbean, Latin American, and South American countries in creating a productive tropical dairy breed. Like the Jersey, the colors are light to dark fawn, with dark nose and hooves. The skin is loose and there is a pronounced dewlap; the breed is horned.

Jersey

The Jersey is a beautiful breed, with a light gray or mouse color that can range to dark fawn. They are smaller than other dairy breeds, but are nervous and have the least docile temperament of the common breeds of cattle. Victorian gentlemen farmers favored the Jersey as a decorative, as well as a productive, animal. The sandy color and deerlike heads made them par-

British breeders gave cattle different names at each stage of development. At birth, the male was called a bull calf, but if castrated it was a bullock. A yearling bull was called a stott if it was castrated. Stotts became steers, bullocks, or oxen. The female calf was called a cow calf, heifer calf, or quey calf. The terms *quey* or *heifer* were used until the first calf was born, when the heifer finally became a *cow*.

Jersey cow with bell

Above: The Jersey is the smallest in physical size of the dairy breeds, and the most variable in color. Some consider the Jersey to be the ideal "family cow," and many Jersey cows will produce a pound (0.45 kg) of butter a day in addition to the milk consumed by the family. (Photo © Lynn Stone)

Jersey cows reflected in stream

Right: As noted by R. M. Gowin 1925 in the American Jersey Cattle Club's official history, *The Jersey Breed: Its Origin, Development and Dairy Value*, "The Jersey cow [is] the highest achievement of the breeder's art, the flower of bovine race; for the dairyman and farmer a perennial source of income; for the lover of pure-bred stock a delight to the eye and a source of abiding interest and pleasure." (Photo © Lynn Stone)

ticularly attractive additions to park-lands.

One of the oldest and smallest of dairy breeds, purebred for six centuries, the Jersey originated on the Island of Jersey, which has been under English rule since A.D. 1204. The small island, only seventy square miles (182 sq-km) in size, is one of the Channel Islands, located on the French side of the English Channel in sight of the coast of Normandy. Farming has been the main industry here, and as a unique and traditional aspect of dairy farming on Jersey, the cows are not pastured. Instead, they are tethered on a short chain and moved several times a day to make maximum use of available grass.

Similar to the Holstein and Guernsey, the Jersey first came to the United States on sailing vessels. In 1853, the famous cow, Flora 113, was noted as having given enough milk during the voyage to produce 511 pounds and 2 ounces (230 kg) of butter.

Kerry

Now a rare breed, the Kerry are thought to be the purest remaining strain of the original Celtic cattle in Ireland from Neolithic times. Named for the Kerry mountains, the cattle are black, with large, lyre-shaped horns and a build typical of cattle used for both dairy and beef. Kerry cattle are known for fiery tempers that make them difficult to keep fenced. One Victorian writer said they were "Truly the poor man's cow, living everywhere, hardy, yielding for her size an abundance of milk of good quality, and fattening rapidly when required."

This breed is still found in Ireland, but although they were imported by into United States beginning in 1818, they have practically disappeared in this country. A few herds exist in Canada. The Irish Department of Agriculture has pledged to support the maintenance of the breed, and numbers are increasing.

Kuri

The borders of Cameroon, Chad, Niger, and Nigeria meet on the shores of Lake Chad, where Kuri cattle are native. White with black points, the Kuri were specifically bred for their large, pear-shaped horns by the Buduma and Kuri tribes who migrated in ancient times from what now are Libya and the Sudan. The Kuri, a docile breed, are kept in herds of thirty cows and one bull, and spend many hours each day swimming in Lake Chad in search of water plants for food. They swim with their heads tilted back so the characteristic buoy-shaped, lightweight horns with spongy interior structure and thin outer shell, act as waterwings. This increases their buoyancy and improves their mobility in the water. In fact, the cattle are so acclimated to water that it's difficult for them to survive away from the Lake Chad area, and they are easily affected by the sun if they're unable to bathe. This makes them unsuitable for many purposes, and although the bulls are friendly and occasionally used as pack animals, they are slow and tire easily. Calves remain with their mothers, and cows are not milked until after the calves are fed, so the cows yield only about one gallon (4 liters) of milk per day.

Limousin

The French Limousin breed has always been bred only for fine beef. Native to the regions of Limousin and Marche, a rugged terrain with rocky soil and a harsh

In the Central African nation of Burundi, more than 80 percent of the people are farmers, and they don't have to depend on clocks for keeping time; they can depend on their cows. "I'll see you tomorrow morning when the cows are going out for grazing," they say. Or if they want to meet in the middle of the day, it's, "I'll see you when the cows are going to drink in the stream," because that's where the cattle are led at midday. Calves are turned out around three o'clock for an evening graze, so "I'll see you when the young cows go out," means let's get together in mid-afternoon.

Limousin calves

Above: In France, these Limousin calves would grow to be called the "butcher's animal." Compared to other European breeds, the Limousin are medium-sized, but their body length and exceptional rumps are their most distinguishing traits and have earned them another nickname: "The Carcass Breed." (Photo © Russell Graves)

Maine-Anjou bull

Right: The Maine-Anjou originated in the northwest agricultural area of France, a region known as the Armorican Peninsula. It is the largest of the French breeds of cattle, with a long, strong back and neck. (Photo © Russell Graves)

climate, the cattle grew to become hardy and resourceful. The region remained relatively isolated for a long time, and farmers developed the breed without genetic interference. Cave drawings at Lascaux, near Montignac, resemble the Limousin, and it is believed the history of the breed may go back at least 20,000 years.

A cross of five-eighths Limousin and three-eighths Brahman creates the Brahmousin. One Brahmousin rancher advertises "A Little Ear & A Lotta Rear," and another claims that "Brahamousin's carcass quality shows even its females: Broody, thick made heifers make long lasting, fertile cows."

Maine-Anjou

Once known as the Mancelle breed, these cattle originated in northwestern France, an area with excellent pasturing and tillable land. The name is taken from the Maine and Anjou River valleys, and it is one of the larger breeds developed in France, where it is known for its easy fattening. In 1843, agriculturist Leclere-Thouin wrote that on the community pastures of the Auge Valley, the Mancelle "were the last to be put onto the grass, but were the first to be picked out to go to the markets in the capital city." Breeders were mostly small farmers, and thus the Maine-Anjou evolved as a dual-purpose breed, with the cows used for milk and the bull calves for beef. Many farms in that area of France still milk Maine-Anjou, and it is not uncommon to find farms where half the cows are milked and the other half raise two calves apiece. The breed was initially introduced to North America in 1969 when the first Maine-Anjou arrived in Canada. They were then brought into the United States through artificial insemination, as was the case with many other European cattle.

Marchigiana

Pronounced *mar-key-jah-nah*, but sometimes called "Markies," this breed is also known by the name Del Cubante. In the fifth century, after the fall of the Roman Empire, barbarians settled in the hilly area of Ancona along Italy's Adriatic coast. These barbarians brought along gray-white cattle from which some think the Marchigiana has descended. Others claim that the Marchigiana is a relatively new breed, becoming known as a distinct breed only in the 1930s when it was locally referred to as the Improved Marche and was developed by breeding Chianinas to two indigenous varieties of mountain cattle. Prior to its recognition as a breed, the Marchigiana was the breed of wealthy landowners outside Rome. Before and during World War I, many of these cattle were moved to the mountains and given over to the care of local farmers so they would not be slaughtered. Even in this different environment, the Marchigiana survived and thrived. Cows are used for breeding until they are ten years of age, at which time they are butchered. After the meat has been frozen and hung for ten days, it is said to be as tender as the meat of a younger animal.

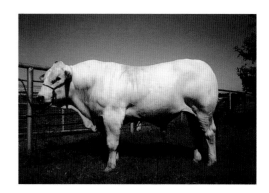

"Dynamite of Red Barn," Marchigiana bull
Sometimes referred to as "Markies," this breed has a natural resistance to insects and heat, and they are popular in Italy where they make up 45 percent of the cattle or cattle hybrids. (Photo © Marky Cattle Association)

Normande cow
The Normande produces rich milk with 4.2 percent butterfat. (Photo © North American Normande Association)

Cotentine
An 1860 illustration of a Cotentine cow, one of several French breeds of cattle that became the foundation for the current Normande breed.

This is an important Italian breed, accounting for approximately 8 percent of the cattle population in Italy.

Murray Grey

Sometimes called the "gentle builders of beef," because they are a mid-sized, relatively docile breed, the Murray Grey originated in New South Wales, Australia, on the Thologolong property of Peter Sutherland. Between 1905 and 1917, one of Sutherland's Shorthorn cows was bred to a variety of Aberdeen-Angus bulls, but she had only gray calves. Sutherland's wife liked the gray calves, so despite the fact that Sutherland felt they would cast a bad light on his black Angus herd, he saved them from slaughter. Peter Sutherland died in 1929, and Mrs. Sutherland sold the gray cattle to her cousin, who started a systematic breeding with eight cows and four bulls.

Through the years, Murray Greys have won beef competitions and are now one of two breeds preferred for Japanese import. In 1969, Murray Grey semen arrived in the United States, and in 1972, a bull calf and yearling heifer arrived. Although growing in popularity in North America, the Murray Grey are fundamentally raised in Australia and New Zealand. Their color is both an asset and a liability—the color reflects heat better than dark colors do, but the inheritance of the color pattern is not well understood, genetically.

N'Dama

Also known by a variety of other names in Africa, this breed is the most representative of the *Bos taurus* breed in West Africa where they currently number approximately 7 million head. N'Dama originated in the Fouta-Djallon highlands of Guinea, and they are naturally trypnotolerant, meaning they are not affected by the tse-tse fly. For the past sixty-five years, the Belgian firm Compagnie J. Van Lancker has developed this breed in Zaire, where it owns 40,000 head of purebred N'Dama. The company has labored to increase the liveweight of the cattle without reducing the breed's hardiness. The firm is working toward an improved genetical analysis and selection of the breed.

Normande

The Normande has its origin in Normandy, where it was brought by Viking conquerors in the ninth and tenth centuries. The breed flourished for a thousand years until the Allied invasion of Normandy during World War II, when the breed was decimated. It has since been revived, and there are currently 3 million Normandes in France. The breed also thrives in South America, where it was introduced in the 1880s. Now flourishing in South America as one of the world's best dual-purpose breeds, numbering more than 4 million cattle and countless Normande crosses, Normandes are raised in Colombia, Brazil, Ecuador, Paraguay, and Uruguay. They are highly adaptable and hardy, and may be found in the Andes Mountains at beef operations located at elevations of 13,000 feet (3,900 meters).

Norwegian Red

This breed is the most popular in the Norwegian national herd. Actually a composite of Ayrshire, Swedish Red-and-White, Friesian, Holstein, Norwegian Red-and-White, Red Trondheim, Red Polled Østerland, and Døle, it is native to Norway, and also known as the *Norsk rødt fe*.

Parthenais

Pronounced *Par-ten-a*, this is a relatively new beef breed in North America, and it is gaining ground in Canada where its popularity is expanding. The Parthenais originated in western Europe, and is a tan, buckskin color with black pigmentation. According to statistics from the French government, this breed produces the high-quality, lean meat preferred by the best restaurants in Paris. The slogan of the French Breed Society is "*Une viande hors du common*," or "A cut above the rest."

Piemontese

The Piemontese, or Piedmontese, is from the Piedmont region of northwest Italy, a secluded area protected by the Alps. The original aurochs were part of this area; then, 25,000 years ago, the zebu (*Bos indicus*) migrated from Pakistan, and part of the migration entered the Piedmont valleys. From the meeting of the aurochs and the zebu evolved the Piemontese breed. In 1886, breeders became aware of double-muscling in the Piedmont breed, a genetic trait that manifests itself as extreme muscling. It is seen infrequently in most breeds, but is now selected for in Piemontese and Belgian Blue, even though the trait has been known to contribute to depressed reproductive performance in females, among other problems.

Pinzgauer

Also known as the Pingau or Jocherg Hummel, the Pinzgauer takes its name from the Pingau district in the province of Salzberg and the Pinz Valley of Austria. The breed developed from cattle belonging to Alpine herdsmen around 500 A.D. The herdsmen were interested in selecting animals from the native red Bavarian cattle that could withstand harsh conditions of the Alps and still produce meat and milk. In the lush valleys of Bavaria, larger, brown and spotted breeds of cattle developed from the same seed-stock. Later, the Pinzgauer attained their unusual present color: a red or mahogany with a white top line that is narrow at the shoulders and wider toward the rump. The tail is white, and white extends over the legs and the underline. Rigid selection for color must have taken place hundreds of years ago. Although the breed did not arrive in Canada until 1972, it gained a firm foothold there and was imported to the United States in 1976, where it has grown in popularity.

Red Sindhi

Native to the Pakistani state of Sind, the

La Vache Qui Rit

The Laughing Cow has been a trademark for cheese from France's Fromageries Bel, Inc., since 1920. According to company spokesmen, the initial artist's rendering was unsatisfactory because the cow looked too happy. The firm called it a *vache hilare*, or "hilarious cow," and believed that it wouldn't sell very much cheese. *La Vache Qui Rit* was an innovative advertising gimmick because prior to 1920 cheese labels usually carried only the name of the manufacturer. With the success of *La Vache Qui Rit*, a herd of "copycows" appeared, including *La Vache Qui Lit* (The Reading Cow), *La Vache Qui Frize* (The Grazing Cow), and *La Vache Qui Fume* (The Smoking Cow).

Norwegian Red milk chocolate

Another kind of "Norwegian Red," this happy cow with her crown of clover is found on a *Cloetta Edel-nott* chocolate bar from Norway.

Piemontese bull and calf
The Piemontese, or Piedmontese, an Italian beef breed, is selected for an unusual genetic trait for double muscling, which provides a generally high yield of meat with a low fat content, without sacrificing quality or tenderness. (Photo © Piedmontese Association of the United States)

Salers cow
The Salers, pronounced *Sa'lair*, is one of the last European breeds to be imported into North America; it has had an influential role in the cattle industry since its introduction in 1975, and has grown by vast numbers ever since. (Photo © Russell Graves)

Pinzgauer cow
The Pinzgauer takes its name from the Pingau district in the province of Salzberg and the Pinz Valley of Austria. Austrians also often refer to a strong, hardworking man as a "Pinzgauer." (Photo © K. Price)

Red Sindhi arrived in Australia in 1954 as a gift to the Australian government. It has become a popular breed in that country and in other parts of Oceania, Asia, Africa, and the Americas due to its adaptability, hardiness, and resistance to ticks and heat.

Romagnola

One of the physically largest breeds of beef cattle, the Romagnola developed from the *Bos primigenius podolicus*, a wild ox from the Italian peninsula, and the *Bos primigenius namadicus*, a breed of bovine from the Euro-Asian steppes that came to Italy during the fourth century with the Gothic invasion led by Aginulf. The Romagnola, therefore, combines the characteristics of both major types of aurochs, and carries lyre-shaped horns (half-moon shaped in bulls), black pigmented skin, and a white or grayish coat. For centuries this breed was used almost exclusively as a draft animal, as "living tractors," but over the past century the characteristics that made them good

workers (muscular loins, rumps, shoulders, and lower thighs) have made Romagnola an excellent source of beef.

Salers

At least 7,000 years ago, Salers were recorded in cave dwellings. Drawings were found by archaeologists near Salers, a small medieval village in central France. They are felt to be one of the oldest and most genetically pure of all European breeds. Originally used for milk, meat, and draft, in the United States Salers are typically used to improve beef cattle, and they are found in almost every state. The Salorn, for example, is a cross consisting of five-eighths Salers and three-eighths Texas Longhorn.

Shorthorn

Shorthorn were initially found on the northeastern coast of England in the counties of Northumberland, Durham, York, and Lincoln. Around 1600, the large cattle in the valley of the Tees River became known as "Teeswater Cattle," but

Senepol cow and calf

Above: The Senepol breed was developed on the Caribbean Island of St. Croix, where N'Dama cattle were imported in the 1880s from Senegal, West Africa. The Senepol evolved from the need to adapt to the tropical environment, as Red Poll genetics were added to the N'Dama, resulting in a breed that lacked the horns of the N'Dama, but improved the milking ability and fertility. The St. Croix herd has had no outside influence due to its isolation and limited genetic base. Senepol breeders advertise "100% *Bos Taurus*; no Brahman, no Zebu." In 1977, the first Senepol were introduced to the United States, but their influence has spread since then across the southern half of the country. This Senepol cow and calf were photographed in Florida. (Photo © Lynn Stone)

Shorthorn cow

Left: The Shorthorn breed is known as the breed of "red, white, and roan," for they may be any one of these colors or combinations thereof. It is also the only breed in North America considered to be a dual-purpose breed, used for dairy as well as beef. (Photo © Russell Graves)

Santa Gertrudis
The Rincon de Santa Gertrudis was the name of the land grant from the King of Spain for the property on which Captain Richard King situated the first headquarters of the famous King Ranch in Texas. The foundation sire of this breed, "Monkey," was named for his antics in the pasture. Even this present day Santa Gertrudis cow can be traced back to Monkey, an exceptional red bull born in 1920 from crosses of Shorthorn and Brahman. The Santa Cruz is another f from the famous King Ranch; both Santa Gertrudis and Santa Cruz involve various combinations of Brahman blood, Angus, Gelbvieh, Red Angus, and Shorthorn. (Photo © Russell Graves)

by the time they were brought to Virginia in 1873 they were known as Durham. The breed became a favorite of the early pioneers, furnishing them with meat, milk, and oxen.

James Herriot's books, documenting his veterinary practice in the Yorkshire hills, revealed that nearly all of his bovine patients were Shorthorns. The breed still holds a favorite place in the dairies of England, and an undeniable influence in other lands as well. The Shorthorn shares with the Friesian the distinction of having had the most widespread and pervasive influence on the world cattle population beyond their native shores.

Today Shorthorns and Milking Shorthorns are found in almost every state in the United States. It is one of the most versatile of breeds, with docile cows that produce large volumes of milk; the beef strain has been influential in the changing needs of the beef cattle industry. It is the only breed in the United States today considered to be a dual-purpose breed.

Simmental

The name *Simmental* comes from the breed's native Simme Valley of Switzerland, *Thal* or *Tal* meaning "valley." A popular breed today, the Simmental is one of the oldest and most widely distributed breeds of cattle in the world. In Switzerland, these red-and-white cattle were prized for their rapid growth, outstanding milk production, and their use as oxen. They became such a popular export that by 1785, the Swiss Parliament had to limit exports to protect their own needs.

Now there are believed to be between 40 million and 60 million Simmental cattle in the world, with more than half this population in Europe.

The Simbrah is a crossbred Simmental with Brahman, developed in the 1960s in the United States. This cross added heat resistance and insect resistance to a breed that was already known for the Simmental's excellent traits.

The Sanhe from Inner Mongolia is a product of natural selection and crossbreeding with the Simmental and Shorthorn. Cows must drink ice water there in winter, the grassland is completely covered with snow for 200 days out of the year, and in summer they are exposed to sunlight and temperatures as high as 51°F (35°C), so the Sanhe fits the need for a rugged, dual-purpose breed.

South Devon

Sometimes called "South Ham," for its bloodline, the South Devon is a combination of the old South Ham and the old Marlborough Red. South Devons are not related to the Devon, but have been a distinct breed since the sixteenth century in the counties of Devon and Cornwall, Great Britain. This is the largest of the British beef breeds, nicknamed "Gentle Giants," for they are docile and universally accepted. The chief characteristic of the South Devon is its yellow-red color.

Sussex

The Sussex is a beef breed that has existed in England since 1066. As British poet Rudyard Kipling (1865–1936) wrote of the Sussex:

There's a pasture in a valley where the hanging woods divide

And a herd lies down and ruminates in peace. . .

On peaceful, postless Sabbaths I con-

Sussex bull
Above: Sussex cows seem to have an inherent instinct for finding water. The cows also have long lives—twelve or more calves per cow are not uncommon.

Simmental cows in the Swiss Alps
Left: These Simmental cattle, named for the Simme Valley of Switzerland, are known in France as Pie Rouge, Montbeliard, or Abondance. In Germany they are called Fleckvieh. And Italy knows the Simmental as Peseta Rosa. (Photo © Lynn Stone)

Tarentaise cow

The Tarentaise is named for the Tarentaise Valley in the French Alps where the breed originated. Over the past century, the Tarentaise have been inbred with other breeds less often than most breeds from France. (Photo © American Tarentaise Association)

sider weighty things—

Such as Sussex cattle feeding in the dew.

Tarentaise

The rugged Savoie region of France, home to the Tarentaise, was the site of the 1992 Winter Olympics. There the breed is used solely for milk production for the making of a Gruyère-type cheese. The average production is 12,199 pounds (5,490 kg) of milk in a 305-day lactation with no fed concentrates in summer. Cows are dried off in fall and kept in the barn from October through April because of snow and the danger of avalanche. Most calving and breeding occurs in winter. In May, the cows are turned out onto lush pastures at 2,500 feet (750 meters). In June, they are moved to high—and extremely steep—pastures at an average elevation of 8,000 feet (2,400 meters). Daily temperatures often swing from below freezing to highs above 80°F (26°C). Grazing ski slopes, the cattle are so removed from any town that the herders actually stay with the cows for the entire three months and make the Beaufort cheese on the spot. Tarentaise are the only cattle in Europe hardy enough to graze this region profitably; climbing at these altitudes is what makes their remarkable natural muscling and marbling, as well as endows the breed with a robust cardiovascular system.

In the early 1900s, the Tarentaise were exported to French colonies in North Africa, where they crossed successfully with indigenous strains of cattle in Algeria, Morocco, and Tunisia. The first Tarentaise in North America were imported to Canada in 1972, and introduced to the United States a year later.

Texas Longhorn

The Texas Longhorn has a complex history. It is not related to British Longhorns used in 1755 by English agriculturist Robert Bakewell in his experiments to establish the concept of "like-breeds-like," but is a separate breed, distinctly American. According to cattle judge Herman Purdy, the Longhorn's earliest ancestors probably accompanied the Moors from Africa to Spain in the eighth century, where they became known as Andalucian cattle and mingled with native European strains. Christopher Columbus brought Andalucian cattle to the Americas on his second voyage in 1493, and left them in the Caribbean port of Santo Domingo, where the breeding herd increased in number. In 1521, during the Spanish Conquest of Mexico, some of these cattle were moved into that country. Conquistador Hernando Cortés stocked his Mexican hacienda, called Cuernavaca, or cow barn, with these cattle from Santo Domingo and Cuba. The cattle multiplied successfully, and by the late 1500s, they had been slaughtered in high numbers for their hides. Only the tongues were kept for food.

From Mexico, the cattle accompanied explorers and settlers into Texas and New Mexico. Coronado took 500 head of Longhorns with him when he searched for the gold-paved "Seven Cities of Cibola" in 1540, a journey that took him as far north as Colorado. The cattle were important to military expeditions and religious missions established in the seventeenth and eighteenth centuries in North America. By 1860, there were 31 million people in the United States, and 26 million cattle counted in Texas. These cattle became known as "Texas Cattle,"

Manure

Question: How does a farmer collect fertilizer?
Answer: All the cows chip in.

Question: What do you get if you stand under a cow?
Answer: A pat on the head.

The average cow produces 30 pounds (13.5 kg) of urine and 65 pounds (29.25 kg) of feces daily, but this varies with the amount of feed consumed and bedding used. Each cow produces at least 15 tons (13.5 metric tons) of manure annually, which consists of 11.4 pounds of nitrogen, 2 pounds of phosphorus, and 10.5 pounds of potassium per ton (5.6 kg of nitrogen, 10 kg of phosphorus, and 5 kg of potassium per metric ton). About 80 percent of the fertilizing value of a feed is excreted in the feces and urine. Cow manure is also a valuable source of organic matter.

Cows deposit their feces in a random fashion and can defecate while walking. This fact is helpful for organizations who sponsor games wherein cows gambol over spaces divided into graphs, and bets can be placed on the numbered spot where a pie will plop. When dry, cow chips provide a lot of fun: An annual Cow Chip Toss is held in Prairie du Sac, Wisconsin, and the longest fling of the bone-dry cookie wins a prize.

The random tendency to poop on the move offers additional jeopardy for devotees of cow-golf played at the Cabot Cow Invitational in Vermont, where hazards are trickier than sand traps or a dogleg. "I think there's something very tranquil about whizzing a golf ball past a heifer's head on a Sunday afternoon," says Anson Tebbets, who opened the course in 1996 on his family's 110-year-old dairy farm. One golfer who hit a hole-in-one admitted, "My secret to success with cow pasture golf is make sure you stare down the cows before you swing." The cows have a tendency to eat the flags, and sometimes nibble the golfers' clothing. "This is an organic golf course," Tebbetts says, "It's only fertilized by Jersey heifers."

The most obvious use for manure is fertilizer, but pigs, who aren't recognized as gourmets, sometimes graze with cows and happily feed on cow dung. In India, cow manure is smeared on the walls of houses and used as plaster; dried manure is used in India as fuel for cooking. In Africa, cattle dung is used for plaster in construction and fuels smudge fires to ward off mosquitoes. Cow urine serves as a principal disinfectant.

Elizabethan England homes were built with exposed beams filled in with a plaster called "wattle and daub," little sticks woven together and slathered with mud and cow muck that still holds up today.

Cow dab is another name for a lump of cow dung. In the past it was burned to repel insects in the United States, but if it was burned as fuel, it was called cow wood.

The average cow's temperature is 101.5 degrees Fahrenheit (38.6 degrees Celsius), but different breeds vary in pulse and respiration.

"Twilight of the Longhorn"
Above: "The twilight of the Longhorn has fallen," author J. Frank Dobie mourned in his book, *The Longhorns* of 1941, and lamented the loss of "a brave and surging part of our national heritage." (Woodcut by Tom Lea)

Texas Longhorn
Right: A Texas Longhorn with the trademark widespread horns. A bit of trivia: Neither bulls nor cows of any breed of cattle will grow the length of horn that steers will. (Photo © Michael Francis)

which meant Longhorns, and hit the trail in 1846 when the first recorded cattle drive from Texas to Missouri took place.

Longhorns wintered in Ohio and were sent to eastern markets in the spring of 1847. Sporadic drives of less than a thousand head took place during the 1850s, and when the Civil War intervened, trail drives were diverted east to supply beef to the Confederacy, with herds swimming the Mississippi River at Vicksburg, Mississippi. After the war, the north was hungry for beef, so northern drives of Longhorn were reestablished. The peak year for the movement of Texas cattle was 1871, when more than 700,000 head were driven north. It was during this period that cow towns, such as Dodge City, Wichita, and Abilene in Kansas, were developed as a result of railroad shipping points for the cattle.

The era that saw 10 million cattle driven from Texas on the Chisolm Trail and other routes lasted only from 1866 to 1890. By the early 1900s, the Longhorn traits were so diluted due to breeding with other cattle that the Longhorn was dangerously close to extinction. Fortunately, the Longhorn herd of old-time Texas rancher Graves Peeler had been maintained pure from the early Mexican cattle, and these served as a notable source of the original Longhorn type. Progeny of this refuge herd continue to thrive in Oklahoma and have provided stock for wildlife preserves, as well as private herds. For the most part, Longhorn cattle are now kept as hobby or curiosity herds, not as commercial beef animals, although a comeback trail is envisioned.

When Longhorn are shown today, they are not shown at halter, in the traditional manner, but are loose in the ring and judged by horseback or buggy.

"The Wooing of Daphnis"

Above: The White Park cattle of Great Britain are an ancient breed, considered holy by the Druids, and are a favorite romantic subject of artists such as Arthur Lemon (1850–1912), who enhanced his painting, "The Wooing of Daphnis," with their presence in this idyllic and appropriately pastoral setting. In classical mythology, Daphnis was regarded by the Greeks as the originator of pastoral poetry.

White Park bull

Right: The White Park—not to be confused with the British White or American White Park—is also historically known as Park, White Forest, White Horned, and Wild White. It is an ancient breed, with a currently critical status. A breeding population of less than fifty White Park cattle exists in the United States, while worldwide, including in its homeland of Great Britain, there are approximately 500 purebred females in seventy-nine herds, plus bulls and young stock. An ongoing breeding program has been organized to ensure the breed's survival. (Photo © White Park Cattle Association of America)

The original Texas Longhorn was a bony animal and varied in color depending on the influence of European breeds. All colors and patterns still appear today. The trademark widespread horns are long and usually upturning, decreasing to a fine point at the end. Older steers of nine or ten years were said to have had horn spreads of up to nine feet (270 cm), but four to five feet (120–150 cm) is probably more accurate for most steers in the cattle-drive days.

Wagu

Actually the word *wagu* means "cattle" in Japanese, and refers to all Japanese beef cattle. The dominant black strains are Tottori, Tajima, Shimane, and Okayama, and the dominant red strains are Kochi and Kumamoto. Most of these breeds were influenced by British and European breeds as much as a century ago, infusing them with Brown Swiss, Shorthorn, Devon, Simmental, Ayrshire, Korean, Holstein, and Angus.

The dominant breed of cattle in Japan is the Japanese Black, representing 86 percent of the country's beef population. When they reach twenty-two months to thirty months of age, Japanese Black heifers are destined to become Kobe beef, a world-famous delicacy. To reach this quality, heifers are fed weighed amounts of feed until their fourth year, when they are sent to professional feeders who put them on a strict diet of crushed and sprouted grain, rice bran, soy beans, chopped rice straw, hay, and grass. They are given regular massages, and every other day they are given a quart (one liter) of beer. The beef resulting from this pampered care is deep red, extremely well marbled, and incredibly expensive.

The original Japanese cows were kept in a stall in the back of the house where they were tended by the farmer's wife and children and regarded as another member of the family. This early breed may still be found southwest of Tokyo in small numbers.

White Park

The White Park cattle of Great Britain were mentioned in pre-Christian Ireland's oral folk stories and figured prominently in the tenth-century laws of the Welsh Prince Hywel the Good. White Park cattle were enclosed in the hunting chases of the Plantagenet kings, and were favorite subjects of famous artists. The Druids chose White Park as their sacrificial cattle.

The White Park are a beautiful breed, with white coats and usually black-colored ears, muzzle, eyelids, feet, and teats. The horns can grow quite long. The upper part of the tongue are black, while the underside of the tongue is usually pink. The intensity of these markings varies from herd to herd.

The origin of the White Park is disputed. Some think they were brought to Britain by the Romans; others feel the Celtic or pre-Celtic White Park type originated on the Iberian peninsula. Many feel the coloration suggests a Scandinavian origin, and they are sometimes confused with the British White or the American White Park, which share common color schemes but are genetically different from the White Park.

During the Roman period in Britain, mention was made of feral herds of horned white cattle. One authority claimed these were the direct descendants of the Wild White Bull that roamed the forests that once covered the British Isles. After the Norman Invasion of 1066, these white herds were rounded up and enclosed in deer parks belonging to the new lords. The herds became a status symbol, and were handed down through generations.

During the seventeenth century, a record of twelve "wild white beasts" were mentioned as existing in Northumberland at Chillingham and also in Durham. Most of today's White Park herds—the Chartley, Dynevor, and Vaynol—are found in the Midlands and north of England. The Cadzow herd is at Cadzow Park in Lanarkshire, Scotland.

In the late 1930s, two pair of White Park cattle were imported into Canada before finding a home in the Bronx Zoo, which lacked facilities to house them for a lengthy period of time. A home was found for them at the King Ranch in Texas, where they remained for nearly forty years. Eventually that herd was sold to a couple in Polk City, Iowa, but it dwindled and was broken up into pieces that went to Big Timber, Montana, and then to Missouri. In 1995, there were five herds of White Park cattle across North America. The breed currently has a critical status, with a worldwide population of less than 200 purebred animals.

Between Alnwick and Berwick-on-Tweed, Great Britain, the Tankerville family's famous wild white cattle, forebears of the White Park breed, have been enclosed on 600 acres (240 hectares) of land where they have been rarely exposed to humans or outside bloodlines since 1250. The only recorded artificial selection has been by the sport of bull-stalking, and by one park keeper who in 1770 deliberately eliminated all the animals with black points, so today the cattle are uniformly red-pointed and lyre-horned, with a whitish coat, red muzzle, and red freckles on the faces and necks of the cows. The horns do not resemble other White Park cattle: they are more upright and curve inwards. Perhaps due to inbreeding, they are not long-lived, with the oldest cows reaching about seventeen years of age and the bulls about thirteen. The herd is now owned and protected by the Chillingham Wild Cattle Association, a registered charity that bought the herd when the eighth Earl died in 1972.

Around the end of the eighteenth century, the breed was used for bull-stalking. As James Wilson described the sport in his *The Evolution of British Cattle* (1909): "The mode of killing them was perhaps the only modern remains of the grandeur of ancient hunting. On notice being given that a wild bull would be killed on a certain day, the inhabitants of the neighbourhood came mounted and armed with guns, etc., sometimes to the amount of an hundred horse, and four or five hundred foot, who stood upon walls or got into trees, while the horsemen rode off the bull from the rest of the herd till he stood at bay, when a marksman dismounted and shot. At some of these huntings twenty or thirty shots have been fired before he was subdued. On such occasions the bleeding victim grew desperately furious, from the smarting of his wounds and the shouts of savage joy that were echoing from every side. But from the number of accidents that happened, this dangerous mode has been little practised of late years, the park-keeper alone generally shooting them with a rifled gun at one shot."

Today the Chillingham herd numbers around sixty head, existing in natural groupings. The cows and young cattle live together with a head bull who is displaced every few years by a successful challenger. The other group consists of mature bulls, who live by themselves.

Zebu

The zebu is not a specific breed but a species of cattle, *Bos indicus*. It was in Brazil and elsewhere in Latin America that all *Bos indicus* breeds became known as zebus, such as the Brahman, or the Nelore, which has the characteristic hump behind the neck. Although Nelore sounds like an Indian breed, the name was given to the Ongole (the breed that contributed most to the Nelore) by Brazil, which has become the largest breeder of the Nelore; Brazil exports these cattle to Argentina, Paraguay, Venezuela, Central America, Mexico, and the United States.

The Ongole originated in India 2000 B.C., when Aryan people brought ancestors of this breed to India, and they became adapted to the extreme environment in that area. The Nelore, on the other hand, arrived in Brazil in 1868, when a ship carrying two Nelores stopped in Salvador, Bahia, on its way to England, and the cattle were sold. In 1878, a breeder from Rio de Janeiro bought two more from the Hamburg Zoo in Germany.

The Nelore, with its hardiness, heat and insect resistance, metabolic efficiency, and maternal instinct and disposition, has proved to be an excellent source of tropical beef production. In the United States, the common spelling is "Nellore," after the name first given to the breed when it arrived in Brazil from its district of origin in Andhra Pradesh. But neither spelling is a synonym for the Ongole breed from Asia.

Another popular zebu type is the Sahiwal, from the dry Punjab region along the India-Pakistan border. A large herd, these cattle were once kept by Junglies, or professional herdsmen. After irrigation was introduced to the area, smaller herds of these cattle could be kept by farmers, who used them for dairy and draft. This is one of the best dairy breeds in India and Pakistan, the heaviest milker of all zebu breeds. In the 1950s, they were introduced to Australia, where they were initially utilized for dairy and beef.

Cow Etiquette

Out in the field, cows may look as if they are just shuffling around haphazardly, but they are actually obeying a set of strict social rules. There is a rigid hierarchy in each herd: Every cow is a queen to all the cows below her, and the fawning subject of the less dominant cows in the herd.

- One cow in the herd bows to none—she's the boss. She has uncontested access to the best pasture, the deepest shade, the choicest spot in the milking line-up, or any other privilege she desires.

- Status seems to depend not necessarily on intelligence, but mostly on the ability to push and shove. Audacity and daring are more important than the capacity for making milk. In fact, high producers are found as often at the bottom as at the top of the social order.

- One poor cow resides at the bottom of the heap. She has no privileges, defends nothing, and takes whatever is left behind or others are willing to share with her. Sometimes she will wait a half hour or more for her turn at the feed bunker rather than start a squabble.

- A cow establishes her rank soon after joining the herd, and once it's set, she is unlikely to be challenged until another newcomer tries to find a place in the social order.

- When feeding patterns are mapped for a herd eating chopped green feed, it has been found that those at the top of the social order walk only about 400 feet (120 meters) and fill up in a little over an hour. Low-status cows walk nearly 1,000 feet (300 meters) and take more than two hours to fill up because of all the shoving around to which they're subjected.

Random Ruminations

I see a cow, and I wonder what it is like to be a cow, and I wonder whether the cow wonders what it is like to be me.
—A. A. Milne, 1920

"It's the eyes," my friend Jim insists. He grew up on a dairy farm, so I figured he could tell me why people are crazy about cows. "Everybody knows if you say a girl has 'cow eyes,' that means she's got big eyes

with long eyelashes. A cow's eyes are really beautiful. It's a compliment!"

Well, I had no idea, but it must have been what Homer (the Greek, not the Simpson) had in mind. In the romantic world of Greek mythology, Homer affectionately called the goddess Hera "Boopis," meaning "cow-faced." There's no record of Hera's reaction to this peculiar sobriquet, but one may assume that "Boopis" as a term of endearment never really caught on. Homer should have explained it was her great big, beautiful eyes.

New Salem Sue, world's largest cow
Facing page: The world's largest cow, New Salem Sue, may be found in New Salem, North Dakota. She's thirty-eight feet high and fifty feet long (11x15 meters), and weighs 12,000 pounds (5,400 kg). (Photo © North Dakota Department of Tourism)

Right: "This is no Bull" postcard

New Zealand postage stamps, featuring major New Zealand cattle breeds.

Singular Sensations

The eyes may have it, but the recent landslide of love and adoration for anything remotely cowlike just seems to get "curiouser and curiouser," as Alice remarked about Wonderland. Cows are making news, hither and yon:

On March 4, 1984, the *London Sunday Telegraph* reported that "Mr. John Coombs, a Wildshire farmer, bald for twenty years, found hairs sprouting again after one of his cows licked the top of his head." He could have made a fortune, but apparently never patented his discovery.

A patent was, however, issued to Alvin Wilbanks, a self-taught engineer from Arkansas who invented a mosquito-repelling machine that will attract and kill mosquitoes in a one-acre (0.4 hectares) radius. According to the *New York Times*, the machine produces a body heat ranging from that of a human to the approximate temperature of a chicken (103–104°F/39–40°C) and "breathes" a moist breeze, which, to a mosquito, smells like cow's breath. "People can't even smell it," Mr. Wilbanks assured a reporter, yet it kills from eight to ten mosquitoes per second.

Another invention worthy of mention is currently being utilized in California, where the cows at George McClelland's dairy farm are contented now, sleeping on comfortable mattresses. McClelland claims milk production is up, diseases are down, and the cows experience bovine bliss as they recline on their three-inch-thick (75-mm) rubber beds, pleasing both the cows, the farmer, and California's animal-rights-sensitive consumers. "See how peaceful and stress-free she looks," McClelland remarked, indicating a Holstein leisurely lying on her bed and chewing her cud.

The special mattresses, made of thick tarp and stuffed with ground-up tires, are made in Ontario and in Vancouver, British Columbia. "Farmers are realizing this isn't some frivolous New Age thing," mattress salesman Joe Shambow says. Farmers in Canada, the eastern United States, and Europe have been using his mattresses for cows for some time, although he's been laughed off an occasional farm when he's tried to show his company's other product: cow air-conditioning. For now, the mattresses are a big success. "They keep those big girls from slipping and falling and banging themselves all up. All we need now is for someone to come up with a cow pillow."

Laughter may be what they're after in Chandler, Arizona, where residents get a kick out of celebrating Doo Dah Days each October, featuring a Great Chandler Moo Off, which is "open to any festivalgoer who is udderly courageous enough to do cow vocals," the local newspaper reports. A parade highlights "Men With Udders," a fashion trend that has yet to catch on anywhere else in the world.

The fashionable fad of body piercing, however, has apparently made an attempt to leap from man to cow. The cover on Aerosmith's 1993 album, *Get a Grip*, pictures an udder with an earring-pierced teat. When cow lovers and animal rights proponents were startled by the bizarre image, the rock and roll band issued a statement explaining that the photograph was manufactured for purposes of the cover illustration only, and no cow teat was actually pierced.

Here's something new and different: You can be the first on your block to have a cow for a pet. There are fifteen minia-

ture breeds from which to choose, and the mini moos are beginning to gain in popularity, according to Dick Gradwahl, the founding director of the International Miniature Cattle Breeder's Society, headquartered in Kent, Washington. If you live on a small farm and want just a little milk or a smaller carcass for beef, Gradwahl's Happy Mountain Miniature Cattle Ranch can provide you with information on the "Oreo Cookie" breed, for example, otherwise known as the Miniature American Beltie, a cross between a Belted Galloway and any other small

breed. Your miniature Oreo Cookie cow will be forty-two inches (105 cm) high or less when it reaches maturity at three years.

Gradwahl has created six new breeds of miniature cattle at Happy Mountain. "It's the newest thing in cattle breeding," Gradwahl assured me. "Perfect for the small-acreage farmer. And the pet cow market is really growing right now. They make great pets. You'd be surprised. Most owners of these great little animals would probably never consider them for beef purposes. Because they're easy to work

Harley-Davidson "Moo-Glide"

Famous for its thoroughbred line of motorcycles, from its early Silent Gray Fellows to its Electra-Glides, Harley-Davidson of Milwaukee, Wisconsin, offered a special edition FLSTN Heritage Softail Nostalgia in the 1990s featuring cowhide insets on the saddlebags and seats. The model quickly earned the moniker "Moo-Glide." Owner: Jim Ference, Lloydminster, Alberta. (Photo © John Dean, Calgary, Alberta)

Lamborghini emblem

Above: Lamborghini automobiles are some of the fastest, most expensive, and most exotic sports cars in the world. Company founder Ferruccio Lamborghini (1916–1993) started building cars in 1963, introducing his famed Miura in 1965. Lamborghini was a bullfighting aficionado, and named the Miura for a famous breed of Spanish fighting bull. The Miura was followed by the prototype Marzal and production Islero, also named for Spanish fighting breeds; the Espada, Spanish for "sword," as used in bullfighting; the Jarama for the Spanish town famous for breeding fighting bulls; and the Urracco, Spanish for "little bull." The now-famous trademark insignia of the charging bull related to Sr. Lamborghini's birthday: He was born under the sign of Taurus.

How to serve the cow . . .

Right: In his treatise on the cow, *How to Serve the Cow*, India's Mahatma Gandhi stated, "We have use for the cow. That is why it has become religiously incumbent on us to protect it." (Photo © Lynn Stone)

with, it's easy to give them names and develop bonding relationships. On our little miniature cattle farm we have Misty, Snuggles, Violet, Nutmeg, and quite a few others. They do produce excellent quality meat, but one piece of advice: If you are going to use one or two for beef, don't give them names."

Have a hankering for a cow of your own, but not enough room to keep one? Good news: You can be a foster cow parent. Get in touch with Stonyfield Yogurt, Londonderry, New Hampshire, and ask for one of their "Have-A-Cow" kits to sponsor your very own cow and receive her suitable-for-framing color photo along with an official, signed adoption certificate with your name and the name of "your" cow prominently displayed. You'll also be sent a personal letter from your cow telling you who her parents are, what her farmers are like, what she eats, and what goes on in her life on the farm.

"My" cow, Shoeless Jo (every heifer in her family has been nicknamed for a baseball player) says her birthday is June 23, which, oddly enough, is the same as mine. A faun-colored, doe-eyed Jersey, Jo lives on Green Wind Farm in Fairfield Vermont. It's no coincidence that Jo is a Jersey—Stonyfield Yogurt and ice cream is made entirely from Jersey milk, "because they produce the highest-protein, sweetest milk around," according to Gary Hirshberg, president of Stonyfield.

Where's the Beef?

In 1860, there were 31,417,331 people in the United States and 25,640,337 cattle, mostly in Texas. Texas still leads the United States in beef production, with 133,000 farms or ranches raising cattle, according to the Agriculture Depart-

160,000 pounds (72,000 kg) of beef weekly. Established by Frank Giuffrida in 1957, the Saugus Hilltop has become a legend in its pursuit of the ultimate filet mignon. A 68-foot-tall (20-meter) green neon cactus marks the original Hilltop on busy U.S. Route 1, and you can't miss the herd of life-sized fiberglass cattle grazing in a corral out in front. A Halloween prank in 1979 found one of the steers on top of the 150-foot-high (45-meter) Great Dome at the Massachusetts Institute of Technology (MIT), but he was soon restored to his rightful place in the Hilltop herd with good humor, along with appropriate mortar board and diploma. The Hilltop cattle are now anchored in cement.

Further west, Rustler's Rooste is perched on top of South Mountain, overlooking the city of Phoenix, Arizona. That's a real, live longhorn steer penned at the entrance to the popular restaurant, where sawdust on the floor, a rustic décor, and live country & western music attempt to whet your appetite for a juicy slab of beef. "Horny," the longhorn out in front, is perhaps not the best advertisement, however. Old-timers on the range used to claim "you could pack all the roasting meat a Texas steer carried in one of his horns," as western author J. Frank Dobie stated in *The Longhorns* (1941).

To wash down all its steaks, The Holy Cow! Casino, Cafe & Brewery in Las Vegas invites you to "Moo for a brew!" The Holy Cow! Brewing Company is Las Vegas's original brewpub, established in 1993. Of course you can get a hamburger (or maybe a beef bratwurst) at the adjacent cafe, and select from a variety of Holy Cow! caps and T-shirts with the Holy Cow! logo—their trademark Hol-

Milking antics
Above: Amish children in Lancaster County, Pennsylvania, practice the age-old trick of spraying milk from the cow's udder. (Photo © Jerry Irwin)

Caught in the act
Left: A farm cat pauses while lapping up a favorite feline treat: fresh milk. (Photo © Bruce Fritz)

ment. All fifty states have beef cattle operations, contributing to a total of 1.2 million dairy and beef cattle farms and ranches in the United States right now.

A recent survey by the National Restaurant Association says beef continues to lead other meats in restaurant sales. The Hilltop Steak House & Butcher Shop in Saugus, Massachusetts, serves more than a million diners each year, and claims, "We have a steak in the beef!" Combined with its sister Hilltop in Braintree, both operations sell at least

stein wearing a pair of red sunglasses to dim the glare of the bright halo hovering over her head. "People have an affinity with the Midwest and with the cow," says owner Tom Wiesner, a native of Wisconsin. He admits that many of his customers are tourists, often from his home state. "You'd think people wanna get away from home, but they go where they're comfortable."

The Grass is Always Greener . . .

Okay, so you love cows, can't get enough of them, but still have a restless desire to see them in a different light. You might consider a visit to Cow Head, Newfoundland. The J&J Hospitality Home bed and breakfast offers reasonable rates, fresh homemade bread, and all the Newfoundland jams you can eat, plus a once-in-a-lifetime chance to post your mail with a "Cow Head" postmark, so how could you go wrong? The modest B&B is run by Dwight and Elizabeth Payne, descendants of the original Cow Head settlers. "The town of Cow Head was settled in 1816 by Paynes from England," Elizabeth writes. "The town consists of a peninsula which we refer to as summerside and the area where the people live which we refer to as winterside. On the western side of the peninsula, facing the ocean, is a rock which at one time looked like the head of a Cow. This is where the name Cow Head originated from. Many years of wear and tear from the raging ocean have changed the shape of the rock. For example, one of the horns have broken off so now it takes a little imagination to picture it looking like a Cow."

It takes less imagination to see a cow in Wisconsin—in fact, they are pretty much taken for granted. The famed

American architect Frank Lloyd Wright (1869–1959) was a native son, and his Taliesen Studio near Spring Green had a working farm on the premises. Wright was outspoken in his personal philosophy about cows: "Wisconsin is a dairy state. That means herds of pure Holsteins or Guernseys, or what have you, occupying the best ground anywhere around, making pictures that go with the one made by the red barn. Wisconsin, fond of passing laws, should pass another law compelling every farmer to paint his barn red. Another that will compel him to pasture his cows by the highway and his pigs back behind the barn."

Colossal Cows

If you find yourself driving through North Dakota you might want to visit New Salem Sue, the World's Largest Holstein. A song has been composed for her, "The Ballad of New Salem Sue," with the lyrics:

> Her presence shows that New Salem
> grows
> With milk-producers' yields;
> We've got the cow, world's largest cow
> That looks across our fields. . . .

In the October 1983 issue of *Outside* magazine, writer Tim Cahill described an actual encounter with this bovine behemoth: "Recently, I drove through North Dakota on the way to visit my parents. I hadn't been in the state for more than ten years and was delighted to discover that there is now a genuine tourist attraction along I-94. Just outside the National Grasslands, I was amazed to see, in the distance, a huge cow standing on a ridge. This cow was at least five miles away, and

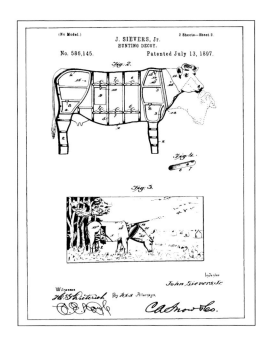

"Trojan cow"
A patent application from 1897 for a hunting decoy shaped like giant cow as invented by one John Sievers, Jr. The hinged head dropped away—presumably so the bovine could graze—allowing the crafty hunter to bag game. A side trapdoor created a blind for a second intrepid hunter.

Feeding calves
Above: Dairy calves are taken from their mothers at birth, and the cows' lactation usually continues for 305 days, assuming a twelve-month calving interval or a two-month dry period before the next calving. (Photo © Jerry Irwin)

Albert, the World's Largest Bull
Left: Standing thirty feet (9 meters) tall, Albert is located in Audubon, Iowa, but must compete with another giant Hereford bull in Pettibone, North Dakota, for his venerable status. And then there are the several statues honoring the legendary Paul Bunyan's mythical companion, Babe the Blue Ox, in the redwoods of Klamath, California, and Bemidji, Minnesota. At least Albert is vocal about his proportions: Push a button near his base and Albert will tell you he's the best.

it dwarfed all the other cows that were standing around in little groups talking about the best way to get out of North Dakota.

"At 80 miles an hour, which is the only way to drive through North Dakota, you stare at that big cow for quite some time before you get to the sign saying that you have been looking at the world's largest Holstein cow. There is a turnoff and an arrow. You can drive right up to the world's largest Holstein cow. My guess, having missed the turnoff, is that the cow was fashioned from ferro-concrete. Clustered about its hoofs were a cafe, a gas station, and perhaps a motel . . . [but] by the time you get to the sign showing you where to turn off to see the world's largest Holstein cow, you've pretty much already seen it."

An equally awesome entity, albeit beefier, the World's Largest Bull, is located in Audubon, Iowa, at the intersection of East Division and Stadium Drive. Albert, a concrete Hereford, stands thirty feet tall (nine meters) and tips the scales at forty-five tons (forty metric tons). He has baby blue eyes and a steelwork frame salvaged from abandoned Iowa windmills. Albert talks, too, but rather immodestly: Push the button and he'll explain that he was built as a replica of the perfect Hereford bull.

As long as you're in Iowa, you might as well catch a glimpse of the Butter Cow, or at least a polystyrene replica of the life-sized cow sculpted from butter that appeared at the 1997 Iowa State Fair; it's at the Des Moines Art Center, and with the push of a button, she will sing a hometown version of "Falling in Love Again."

Cow poetry

"Cow Poetry"
Far Side creator Gary Larson has long been enamored with the bovine species. (THE FAR SIDE © 1990 FARWORKS, INC. Used by permission of UNIVERSAL PRESS SYNDICATE. All rights reserved)

Les Vaches
Dutch Impressionist painter Vincent Van Gogh's (1853–1890) oil painting of *Les Vache*, or "The Cows." (Musée des Beaux-Arts, Lille, France)

"All the Good Ideas"

American artist Andy Warhol (1927–1987) began as a commercial illustrator, but his iconoclastic silkscreens made him one of the leading figures of the Pop Art movement and an internationally recognized symbol of modern art. The Andy Warhol Museum in Pittsburgh, Pennsylvania, offers an entirely different perspective on bovine beauty: The fifth floor contains an entire room wallpapered with the famed artist's rendering of a cow's head. Warhol had apparently given up painting in the mid-1960s, when he turned his talents to producing films and promoting the rock group The Velvet Underground. For his second exhibition with Leo Castelli, a leading dealer of contemporary art in New York City, Warhol created two rooms: Silver Clouds, containing helium-filled balloons that moved with currents of air; and Cow Wallpaper, an environment covered with, well, cow wallpaper.

Joe Fafard, one of Canada's best-known contemporary artists, has produced numerous sculptures of livestock that have found homes in Canada, the United States, and Europe. An entire herd of cattle—seven cows at rest—can be viewed in an exterior installation entitled "The Pasture," on permanent display at the Toronto Dominion Centre since 1985. Known for the spontaneity of his

Barnyard, 1900
People and cows lived close together in the barnyard on the pioneer homestead of Rolla B. Shufelt near Oconto, Wisconsin. (State Historical Society of Wisconsin)

"The Pasture"
Canadian artist Joe Fafard brought the prairie to the city in his 1984–1985 sculpture installation, "The Pasture," in downtown Toronto, featuring six larger-than-life bronze bovines reposing on a patch of grass amid the skyscrapers of the financial district. The cows were also featured at the Montreal Museum of Fine Arts retrospective of Fafard's work, "The Bronze Years," in 1996–1997. (Photo © Brian Merrett. Courtesy of the Montreal Museum of Fine Arts and Susan Whitney Gallery, Regina, Saskatchewan)

Monument
Above: Statues of a Holstein cow and calf pay homage to this dairy farm's producers. (Photo © Bruce Fritz)

"Foster Mothers of the Human Race"
Left: Bovine postcard of the "five dairy queens"—from left: Brown Swiss, Ayrshire, Holstein, Guernsey, and Jersey—from *Hoard's Dairyman*.

Miniature Hereford bull

Dick Gradwahl, founding director of the International Miniature Cattle Breeder's Society, with "Happy," a miniature Hereford bull who stands forty-two inches (105 cm) tall at thirty-seven months.

It takes 340 squirts of milk to fill a milk pail, according to research carried out by Allen Staigler of Edgar County, Illinois, who milked ten to seventeen cows by hand twice a day for fifteen years and had plenty of time to contemplate his squirts.

---

work and the sense of western Canada incorporated in his art, Fafard's bronze bovines were displayed in a massive retrospective collection, "The Bronze Years," at the Jean-Noël Desmarais Pavilion in 1996. The artist has his own foundry, Julienne Atelier Inc., in Pense. Fafard has lived and worked in Regina since 1987.

Fafard may agree with the statement of the American artist Grant Wood (1892–1942) who said, "All the good ideas I ever had came to me while I was milking a cow." Wood's fondness for cows was borne out by a statement made by architect Ludwig Mies van der Rohe, a guest of Wood at a ranch in Wyoming in 1937. Van der Rohe wrote, "on a ranch one must do something, so Grant Wood said, 'I will milk a cow,' and every morning for three days he milked her. Then he tired of the cow, so for two mornings he did nothing. The third morning a noise came at his bedroom window and there was the cow. 'See?' he said, 'Now she comes to me.'"

An artist of another sort, cartoonist Gary Larson, has featured cows in many of his favorite cartoons for years. "I don't know what clicked the first time I drew a cow. It was enjoyable. There's something even funny in the name itself. I found myself gravitating toward it in different ways. Excessively, I think now."

Thoroughly Cowed

Curiosity may have killed a cat, but it only enhances the natural instinct of the cow. Stand next to a fence, as I did out at Jack Goodman's ranch near Buhl, Idaho, last fall, and the inquisitive herd will venture as close as possible to look you up and down. In this case, the cattle were tiny black Dexter cattle, native to Ireland; now there are only about a thousand Dexters in the world, a "curious" breed indeed. "Come Bos, Come Bos," my husband murmured, trying to induce a little heifer to nibble a handful of hay from his hand. "Do you know why you call them *Bos*?" I almost asked before I bit my tongue (I've learned the hard way, a little trivia goes a long way with one's family). But in case you've ever wondered, it's because cows are of the genus *Bos*. That's why so many cows are named "Bossy."

When you think about it, the really curious thing about cows is that folks who never may have seen a real cow possess prized collections of cow mugs, creamers, cookie jars, potholders, salt and pepper shakers, cow doo dads, and cow duds. Even Madeleine Albright, Secretary of State in the Clinton Administration, has a Virginia farm decorated with a cow motif, with bovine potholders and figurines adorning the kitchen where she cooks.

Ruminating on all of this cow material, I was paging through a pet catalog the other day, and found myself confronted with a photo of "Pig Snooters and Beefy Wafers," made from freeze-dried hog and beef snouts, "a treat for the pet that craves variety." Other delicacies included "Moo Tubes, hickory basted wind pipes or tracheas slowly roasted in

Cowboy of today
Above: A modern-day cowboy carries a calf to be doctored at the Hilger Cattle Company ranch near Dodd City, Texas. (Photo © Russell Graves)

Cowgirl of yesterday
Left: A Wyoming cowgirl rides the range in this watercolor by cowboy artist E. W. "Bill" Gollings (1878–1932).

Q. What has four legs and flies?
A. A cow in summer.

Back in the Saddle Again: Cowboy Daze

Without the cow there would have been no cowboy, no John Wayne westerns, no Roy Rogers and Trigger, no Gene Autry singing "Tumbling Tumbleweeds." In truth, the Texas Longhorn cattle drives spanned only a slim period of years, from 1866 to 1890, but the romance of the rugged cowboy and our love affair with that era in history has fascinated us for decades and is certain to last forever.

According to an old saying, "All it took to make a cowman was a rope, nerve to use it, and a branding iron."

The Spanish word *caballero* means "horseman." *Vaquero* means "the mounted worker with cows," or "cowboy." The name for Cuernavaca, Mexico, means "Cow Horn." During the days of the great cattle drives, it cost about a dollar a head to drive an average herd of cattle from southern Texas to the far Northwest. If a cow dropped a calf during a cattle drive, the calf was shot so the cow could move on without the wobbly calf tagging along and slowing down the herd. Later, a "calf wagon" was driven with the herd, to pick up calves born on the trail. But a half-dozen or so calves jostling together during the day would get their scents mixed up, and the mothers wouldn't recognize them at night. This was resolved by baptizing the calf in the cow's urine. If a cow lost her calf and at the same time there was a calf that had lost its mother, the bloodless hide of the dead calf was fastened over the orphan so the cow would adopt it and let it suckle.

Before it was admitted to the United States in 1850, cattle breeding was the only remunerative occupation in California. At the time, the value of cattle lay solely in the worth of their hides and their tallow. In the 1870s, many early colonists thought the Texas Longhorn was indigenous to the land. Some called them "mustang cattle," or "Spanish cattle," but a common description was simply "wild cattle." After the American Civil War, they were known as "Texas cattle," and eventually they became known as "Texas Longhorns."

During the early days of the United States, Longhorn cattle were hunted as game animals. Following the American Civil War, one military man commented that, "It is much more difficult to get a shot at a wild Texas cow than it would be at the most cautious and wary old buck."

Two sets of Longhorn horns with a nine-foot (270-cm) spread were to be seen at the Columbian Exposition of 1893 in Chicago. Because horns contain the essence of glue, they can be steam-heated or boiled and straightened, so a certain amount of curve is transformed into horizontal length.

According to J. Frank Dobie's *The Longhorns* (1941), "probably ninety per cent of North American cattle are branded on the left side. The practice of so branding them may be based on the inclination of cattle to pull to the right, leaving the 'brand side' out for a view."

Cowboy
An engraving of the mythical American cowboy created by famed artist Frederic Remington in the late 1800s.

The word *maverick,* for a stray or an unbranded animal seen on the range (as in "Yonder goes a maverick") is possibly derived from Samuel Maverick, who did not brand or earmark any of his cattle. Thus, when other ranchers who branded their herds saw an unbranded animal, they determined it must be "One of Mr. Maverick's animals." In 1861, legend says that Samuel Maverick was the largest landholder in the United States and owned more cattle than any other man in Texas. Another legend claims that Maverick had nothing except "an old stag, a branding iron, a tireless perseverance, and a morality that was blind in one eye," Dobie wrote in *The Longhorns* he became "one of the cattle kings" and was the bull of the woods in "bovine aristocracy." Actually, Samuel A. Maverick, a lawyer, was one of the signers of the Texas Declaration of Independence against Mexico, and an extensive speculator in lands. Unfortunately, the term *mavericking* eventually became a synonym for stealing. Mavericks would sometimes slit the tongue of a sucking calf so it could no longer suck and would stop following its mother. Also, if a calf with a slit tongue were put in a pen with other calves, it could not bawl and betray its presence in the strange place.

In contrast to the horse, whose hair slopes backward toward the rump, the cow's hair slopes forward toward the head. This curious oddity is apparently responsible for the fact that cows on the open range would move forward with the wind during a storm. After the great prairie blizzards, hundreds of cows were sometimes found piled up dead in a box canyon or lined at the base of the cliffs they had wandered over. Horses, on the other hand, simply turned and faced the wind.

Stampede is from the Spanish *estampida*, but the old Texan word was *stompede,* and the wild and nervous Longhorn cattle did it often. Greek herdsmen called it "panic terror." One Texas old-timer defined a stampede as "one jump to their feet and another jump to hell."

There was a saying that if you could drive a herd for two weeks without a stampede, the danger was over. Thunder and lightning were the most common cause of stampedes, and cattle usually stampeded at night. The next most frequent cause was the scent of wolves.

Nearly all the old authentic cowboy tunes to soothe the herd had a slow tempo, as slow as a horse walking around sleeping cattle at night. The old cowboy song, "I'm a-Leading Old Dan," described the jittery Longhorn's tendency to stampede with the lines:

Ride around the little dogies, O ride around 'em slow,

For the fieries and the snuffies are a-raring to go.

Cattle drive
Cowboys drive a herd of Texas Longhorn down the main street of Dodge City, Kansas, the cattle capital of the Wild West. This fanciful engraving appeared in *Frank Leslie's Illustrated Newspaper* in 1878.

Holstein home
No, you're not seeing spots. This home in Oregon is painted from top to bottom and all around in Holstein colors. Even the mailbox wears black and white spots. (Photo © Randy Leffingwell)

"Eulogy on the Cow"
by Nat Curran, 1945

Tho eulogies are penned perforce
In honor of the dog and horse,
The cow excels them definitely
In matters of fidelity.
In winter wind or summer breeze
She labors for our milk and cheese,
And scientific tests have shown
She puts the ice cream in the cone.
When in Elysian fields she rests,
She leaves us numerous bequests—
Wallets, gelatins and shoes,
soaps and pocketbooks and glues;
Bequeaths her very bones, indeed,
To pulverize for poultry feed.
The briefcases she leaves behind
Protect the plans of humankind.
And belts—her halo and her crown—
She keeps our pants from falling down.

their own juices for a protein-rich taste that is unlike any other." I'll bet. Cows chew their cud; dogs are now encouraged to munch on cows' ears, noses, hooves, and innards. Somehow that seemed incongruous.

Indeed, we owe the cow our gratitude for the milk in our baby bottle and the beef in our Big Mac, but there's also a vast array of products today that you'd never imagine came from a cow, like collagen for plastic surgery, heparin for blood clots, vitamin B-12—all of these because cattle are organically similar to humans, so our bodies easily accept medication or treatments made with their components. Cattle fats and proteins provide everyday household products like candles, cosmetics, paints, paper, and perfume. Then there are crayons, deodorants, detergents, floor wax, insecticides, insulation, linoleum, mouthwash, shaving cream, soaps, toothpaste . . . had enough, yet? Anti-

freeze contains gycerol, derived from fat. Asphalt contains a binding agent from beef fat. Automobile and jet lubricants are made from beef fats and proteins, as are outboard-engine oil, high-performance greases, and brake fluid. Even tires have stearic acid, helping rubber hold its shape.

The truth is, humans can use about 99 percent of the cow. Cattle contribute significantly to almost every facet of our lives. We really do consume nearly everything but the *moo*.

Urban Cow Legend
No matter how you encounter a cow, unexpected emotions may arise. In 1995, the *Manchester Guardian* of Manchester, England, ran a story entitled, "Falling Cow Sinks Ship?"

It seems a fisherman was minding his nets on the Caspian Sea one day when a cow fell out of the sky and plunged

Cow quilt
A quilted barnyard scene from Lancaster, Pennsylvania. (Photo © Keith Baum/Courtesy of Sunflower Foundation Quilts)

U.S. President Zachary Taylor (1849–1850) died in office after serving only sixteen months of his term. Doctors said his death was the result of drinking cold milk after eating cherries on a hot day.

"Coretta and Anita"
Canadian artist Joe Fafard's bronze bovine sculptures stand like timeless spirits on the prairie. (Photo © Don Hall. Courtesy of Susan Whitney Gallery, Regina, Saskatchewan)

through his boat. With one fell swoop, the fisherman's livelihood was destroyed, and his insurance did not cover plummeting cattle. The fisherman's story provoked chuckles in the Urals, but he had the last laugh when he was given a new boat, courtesy of the U.S. Embassy in Moscow, which accepted full responsibility. According to the *Guardian*, a United States Air Force plane "was on a famine relief mission when one of the heifers on board went berserk at 3,000 feet, knocking a squaddy unconscious and dribbling on an officer's trousers. In their apoplexy, the soldiers decided the dumb animal had to take a dive. So they opened the cargo door and gave the poor cow the

heave-ho out into the wide blue yonder."

Amazingly, that same story has been translated by the German Embassy in Moscow into a tale of Russian cows falling onto a Japanese fishing boat. In their version, Russian soldiers stole a couple cows and transported them via plane, but the cattle got out of control, and the crew tossed them out in order to avoid a crash.

Russians say the falling cow story is similar to a long-standing joke in which a Russian fisherman blames the loss of his boat on a falling cow. But the adventure also bears similarity to an episode in a popular recent Russian film and bestselling video, *Osobennosti Natsionalnoi Okhoty* ("Peculiarities of the National

How to Name Your Cow

By Roz Gausman

Naming a cow can be as simple as giving her a number. On our farm in the town of Dunn in Dane County, Wisconsin, the cows get numbers—although most of them get names, as well. We spend more time with these girls than most people spend with their coworkers, so it is nice to personalize them.

Most of their names just fall into place based on their personality or a certain characteristic of the cow, her parents, a previous owner, or even a relative of the current owner. There probably isn't a farm around that hasn't had a cow named "Kicker," "Stubby Tail," or "Aunt Mary"—named after either the farmer's favorite or worst aunt, depending on the personality of the cow and the aunt.

We also have cows with names that needed an explanation, like "Miss Piggy," who was the dirtiest cow in the herd. "Dolly" is named after Dolly Parton for certain features other than a blonde wig or singing country music. "Who" has a perfect question mark on her nose, and "Checker" has a check mark on her forehead. Then there was "Sonny," short for Son of a Bitch, because she would kick the milking machine off, or, worse yet, squeeze in front of the stanchion and break off a water cup.

Occasionally a cow would be purchased and she was either given the name of someone in the previous owner's family so we could remember where she was from, or she was given a name by her previous owner, such a "Meathead," which we soon discovered was their equivalent to our "Sonny" because of her temperament.

Farms with registered cows may have a "Daisy," "Bess," or "Elsie," and that name is likely a nickname for one of the many names on her pedigree registration indicating her bloodline, such as "Selwood Betty's Commander," or "Sunny View Improved Serenity." Our farm has grade cows instead of registered, but we still end up passing on some name recognition between generations. For instance, "Meathead" was with us for many years, despite her temperament, and she gave us several heifers, which we named "Jughead," "Whitehead," and "Blackhead."

All of our cows have identification numbers, which they are given at birth. But the ways for numbering cows vary as much as naming them. We use eartags and necktags with the same number, so if the cows lose one they still have the other. We change the color of tags each year and just number the calves in the sequence they arrive. Another method used in numbering is to start with the number of the year, then the calf number. For instance, cow 722 would be the twenty-second calf born in 1997.

Getting a number is a sure thing, but getting a name is not always guaranteed. A name is earned; it's a privilege. The unnamed cows are referred to by their numbers until they are lucky enough to get a name. The names of our cows are always a topic of discussion with farm visitors. Young visitors to our farm are always honored when we ask them to help us name one of our no-name cows. Most of them choose their own name to give the cow, but some, like our neighbor's grandson, put a lot of thought into it before coming up with the name "Milkgirl."

Q. What is the most important use for cowhide?
A. It holds the cow together.

BLAME IT ON THE BOSSY NOVA

Bossy Nova
Bovine cartoon by New York artist Ken Brown.

Flatulo Ergo Bovum: I Fart Therefore
I am a Cow. (Latin)

Hunt"), which depicts hunters hiding a stolen cow inside a military jet.

The True Spirit of Moo

Sometimes a cow will enter your world when you least expect it, and the eventual outcome will change your life. That's what happened to Judy and Ron Magnusson, in the upper Chumstick Valley of Washington. The Magnussons were visited by Missy Cow Cow, a half-ton (450-kg) Red Angus and Hereford cross. According to Judy Magnusson, it happened like this:

"Some six or seven years ago, Missy Cow Cow was bought at an auction house by the Alpine Boy's Ranch. When it came time to unload her at the ranch's barbed wire pasture, she just kept going and ran through the fence. The ranch is a good six and a half miles by highway from our home. Missy Cow Cow never went toward the highway, though; she lived in and on the steep mountains that are between the ranch and us. Men on horseback spent many days looking for her. The hunters in fall were always on the lookout for her, as well, but they never spotted her. She must have learned from the deer how to eat and blend into the surroundings.

"Our twenty acres is seventeen acres of steep, rocky and treed, with a good three acres of grassland where our homesite sits. In 1991, I had planted a veggie garden. I thought it was an elk that was eating my cabbage, squash plants and beets, with only the hoofprints to show

what had been there during the night. We never got to see her until 1993, when she went walking down our driveway one day. I assumed she belonged to our neighbors, but a phone call proved me wrong.

"We put out a five gallon bucket of water for her some hundred feet from the house, along with a salt lick. She feasted then on the wild grasses, elderberry trees, choke cherry trees, and the vine maple trees, sometimes chewing away at a branch that was at least an inch in diameter. She only made rare appearances then, but in 1994 she came more often. The times we spotted her, we would just go out on our deck and start talking to her. You know, things like, 'Hi, you big cow. Missy Cow Cow come for some water? Oh, Missy Cow Cow come closer so I can get a picture of you!'

"That year at the end of July, a firestorm broke out, threatening our twenty acres. Firefighters told me it was time to leave because the fire was within a mile of our home. As I left with my two dogs and cat I asked the firemen if they would keep Missy Cow Cow's water bucket full for her. She emptied it, but they never did see her. When we returned I called for her, and it was then I knew she knew my voice and her name stuck! It was then she let me touch her, as long as our dog, Keeta, was nearby—a Malamute-coyote-Shepard mix. They had become friends.

"At the start of winter 1994 we bought a fifty pound bag of alfalfa pellets and fed her only at dusk, when she came to the window and put her nose on the pane and moooed. Nineteen ninety-five came, and she was here all the time. She was fast becoming a pet, letting me brush her from head to tail, as long as

Q. What do you call a cow that has just had a calf?
A. A de-calfinated cow.

Mother love
A Hereford cow cleans her calf. (Photo © Bruce Fritz)

Missy Cow Cow
Above: Missy Cow Cow rests in the front yard of Judy and Ron Magnusson of Chumstick Valley, Washington. (Photo © Judy Magnusson)

Holstein in buttercups
Facing page: An old superstition, that cows eat buttercups to help them produce better butter, has not been scientifically proven. (Photo © Bruce Fritz)

"A dessert course without cheese is like a beautiful woman with one eye."
—Anthelme Brillat-Savarin (1755–1826)

Keeta was there. Soon Missy Cow Cow began to leap and run alongside the driveway as Keeta and I walked down to the highway to get our mail, and again in the afternoon for the newspapers. By that fall we were buying alfalfa pellets regularly and feeding her twice a day. By winter of '96 we added additional feed, until the first of April, when she took a liking to my pansies and our fruit trees."

The winter of 1996–1997 was harsh in Chumstick Valley, and the Magnusson farm was surrounded by four feet (120 cm) of snow. Missy Cow Cow became trapped by the deep snow around the house and spent the entire winter near a space the family cleared by the front door. Her main exercise was walking up and down the plowed driveway. By spring, the front yard was a mass of cowpies (spread on Judy's garden), but neighbors began to complain that the cow was a nuisance, causing erosion and eating gardens, nibbling at yards. The Magnussons had no choice but to have Missy Cow Cow put down.

"I couldn't face it," Judy says, "I could never eat her on my dinner plate." The Alpine Boys Ranch agreed to take the meat and pay for Missy Cow Cow to be cut and wrapped, and professionals with guns were summoned.

"I'd already left, because I didn't want to see it, but my husband stood there with her, and he said it was the hardest thing he'd ever done. He stood there petting her, and they shot her once, and it didn't do anything, didn't even draw blood, so they shot her two more times. The third bullet hit her dead center on the side where her brand is, and it just bounced off her. Maybe it was the sting, but by that time she'd had enough and just trotted off into the mountains without even a limp."

It took a long while for Missy Cow Cow to respond to Judy's calls after the fiasco with the marksmen. Finally, however, the cow timidly returned to the yard, and a newspaper story about Missy Cow Cow in the local *Wenatchee World* brought calls for adoption of the indomitable bovine. The Magnussons waited until they could be sure of a home that would let her live out her normal life. Now Missy Cow Cow's home is the Wild Burro Rescue Ranch, in Onalaska, Washington, but Judy says she and her husband miss her a lot.

"Lately I've been trying to detach myself, but she's such a beautiful animal. Whoever would have thought that I'd have a pet that big? She was refreshing, a bright spot in what just happened to be many dark, emotional, stress-filled moments of our lives. I am a Christian, and I have firmly believed since Day One that Missy Cow Cow was God's cow, and He sent her here to make us aware that He could use Missy Cow Cow to bring joy, peace, and love through one of his creations. Psalms 50:10 says, "For every beast of the forest is mine, and the cattle upon a thousand hills.' I would like to think that our hill is one of the thousand!"

Cow figurines
A sample of the many cow figurines from the collection of Richard Bohn of Lancaster, Pennsylvania. (Photo © Keith Baum)

Termites out-gas cattle in methane production: In 1971, during a debate over the deleterious effects of supersonic transports on the stratosphere, it was revealed that bovine flatulence sent an estimated 85 million tons (76.5 million metric tons) of methane into the atmosphere each year. But more recently, scientists discovered that termites digesting decaying vegetable matter actually produce 150 tons (135 million metric tons) of methane a year and more carbon monoxide than all the smokestacks in the world.

Memories of a Former Kid

By Bob Artley

For several decades now, artist Bob Artley has collected his reminiscences of farming life into a syndicated cartoon series entitled "Memories of a Former Kid" that originated from the *Worthington Daily Globe* newspaper in Worthington, Minnesota. His drawings and essays have also been collected into several books, including *Memories of a Former Kid*, *A Book of Chores As Remembered by a Former Kid*, and *Living with Cows*.

Artley's love-hate relationship with the bovine species began as a child who learned firsthand how to milk Bossy. "Cows are high on the list of our fellow creatures for which I feel a genuine affection," he says. These four drawings depict the trials and tribulations—as well as the joys—of living with cows as recounted by a former kid.

Weather Cows

Cows may be able to forecast the weather. Scientists attribute certain changes in the behavior of cattle to the lowering pressure preceding a storm system.

Cows may refuse to graze if they sense an impending storm, and will lie down.

Cows may bunch together before a storm hits and move down from the crests of hills into sheltered valleys.

Cows sometimes huddle beneath trees if they sense the storm to be a short one and, as a result, have been struck by lightning.

If cows lie down early in the morning, it will rain before night.

When cattle stand with their backs to the wind, rain is coming.

When cows refuse to go into the pasture in the morning, it will rain before night.

If a bull leads the cows going out to pasture, anticipate rain.

If a cow carries her tail upright, rain is approaching.

If a cow slaps her tail against a tree or a fence, it is a sign of bad weather ahead.

In Yorkshire, England, children sing cow-charms about the weather. At the first snow of the year they chant:
  "Snow, snow faster, the cow's in the pasture."
  And when they've had enough snow, they sing:
  "Snow, snow, give over, the cow's in clover!"

The best known sign of an imminent earthquake is extreme restlessness on the part of domestic animals, especially cattle.

"The Purple Cow"
by F. Gelett Burgess, 1895

I never saw a purple cow,
I never hope to see one;
But I can tell you, anyhow,
I'd rather see than be one!

Riding into the sunset
A Texas Longhorn stands silhouetted by the evening sun on the Hope Ranch near Bonham, Texas. (Photo © Russell Graves)

Bovine Reading and Reference

Thomas Jefferson introduced ice cream, waffles, and macaroni to the United States.

Alderson, Lawrence, and Robert Dowling. *Rare Breeds: Endangered Farm Animals*. Boston: Bulfinch Press, 1994.

Amoroso, E. C., and P. A. Jewell. *Man and Cattle*. N.p.: Anthropological Institute of Great Britain and Ireland, 1963.

Breeds and Breeders: A Guide to Minority Livestock Breeds in Canada, 1992. Joywind Farm, Rare Breed Conservancy.

Briggs, H. M., and D. M. Briggs. *Modern Breeds of Livestock*. Fourth ed. Macmillan Publishing Co., 1980.

Conway, D. J. *Animal Magick: The Art of Recognizing and Working with Familiars*. St. Paul, Minn.: Llewellyn Publications, 1995.

Dobie, J. Frank. *The Longhorns*. Boston: Little, Brown & Co., 1941.

Gallico, Paul. *Ludmila: A Legend of Liechtenstein*. New York: Doubleday & Company, Inc., 1959.

Genus Bos: Cattle Breeds of the World. Rahway, N. J.: Merck & Co. Inc., 1985.

Heck, Lutz. *Animals, My Adventure*. Trans. by E. W. Dickes. London: Methuen & Co. Ltd., 1952.

Krutch, Joseph, ed. *The World of Animals: A Treasury of Lore, Legend and Literature by Great Writers and Naturalists from the 5th Century to the Present*. New York: Simon and Schuster, 1961.

Lucas, A. T. *Cattle in Ancient Ireland*. Kilkenny, Ireland: Boethius Press, 1989.

Mason, I. L., *World Dictionary of Livestock Breeds, Types and Varieties*. Fourth ed. C. A. B. International, 1996.

Porter, Valerie. *Cattle: A Handbook to the Breeds of the World*. Facts on File Publications, 1992.

Prose and Poetry of the Live Stock Industry of the United States. Denver, Colo.: National Live Stock Association, 1904. Facsimile edition: New York: Antiquarian Press, 1959.

Pukite, John. *A Field Guide to Cows*. Helena, Mont.: Falcon Press, 1996.

Purdy, Herman R. *Breeds of Cattle*. New York: Chanticleer Press, 1987.

Rath, Sara. *About Cows*. Minocqua, Wisc.: NorthWord Press, 1987.

Seuling, Barbara. *The Last Cow on the White House Lawn & Other Little Known Facts About The Presidency*. New York: Doubleday & Company, Inc., 1978.

Tudor, Alice M. *A Little Book of Birds & Beasts*. London: The Medici Society, Ltd., 1929.

Van Wagenen, Jared, Jr. *The Cow*. New York: The Macmillan Company, 1922.

Wilson, James. *The Evolution of British Cattle*. London: Vinton & Co. Ltd., 1909.

Index

About the Author

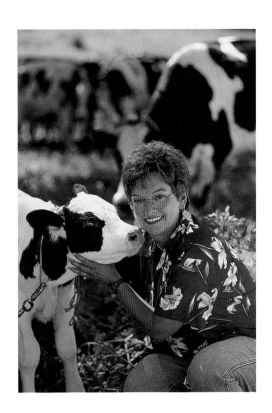

This is Sara Rath's eighth book and complements her award-winning 1987 publication, *About Cows,* which has enjoyed worldwide success. Sara was born and raised in Manawa, a small town in central Wisconsin—her grandfather was World Champion Cheesemaker for many years—and the rural landscape of the Midwest is central to her poetry and fiction. She has received numerous awards, including a Wisconsin Arts Board Fellowship and fellowships from the MacDowell Colony and Ucross Foundation. Sara and her husband, Del Lamont, reside in Elm Grove, Wisconsin.

Author Sara Rath with a newborn Holstein calf on the farm of Rosalyn and Bill Gausman in the town of Dunn, Dane County, Wisconsin. (Photo © Bruce Fritz)